JOSHUA DIMOND

Neighborhoods Uncovered

How local real estate investors get the edge on finding top performing markets and pricing strategies to maximize profits

First edition

This book was professionally typeset on Reedsy.
Find out more at reedsy.com

Contents

Overview

If the number 1, 2, and 3 rules in real estate are Location, Location, Location, why are there so few people teaching you how to truly find the best locations for real estate? Despite the numerous books written with the purpose of teaching the local real estate investor how to invest in real estate, very few of them provide a road map as to *where* the local investor should invest. This book finally solves that issue by teaching the local investor how to uncover the top investment neighborhoods across the nation; creating a consistent, repeatable, customizable process allowing the local investor to not just identify the best market in the country to invest in, but more importantly, the best market for *them* to invest in.

This book will walk you through how to define what the best location is based on property trended valuations, quantifiable economic indicators, and qualitative demand characteristics. Whether you're looking to fix and flip a single family home or rent out a 20 unit apartment complex and everything in between; I will walk you through how to identify the "hottest" growth markets, to the historically best performing long-term buy and hold markets.

It's always frustrating to me when you search through Amazon or other online resources for books on "real estate market analysis" or "how to find the best locations to invest in," you mainly find overpriced textbooks with limited real-world applicable examples for local investors. The most relevant and relatable non-textbook I found was from 2010. It had some decent reviews but contained mainly paid-for resources not geared for the local investor either.

Simply Googling "hot real estate markets," or "how to find the best real estate investment markets," I have only ever found the same headline stories providing nothing useful for any real estate investment. Someone telling a local investor the "Top 5 Cities to invest in nationally" is usually not helpful given most local investors start in their state. It does not help to tell someone in San Francisco that Nampa City, Idaho is the best market to flip houses or coming up with a top-five national list of the most expensive markets and least expensive to flip in. If your market is expensive, you know it is expensive. The important part is: does the deal offset those expenses?

The bottom line, there is a significant knowledge gap in being able to identify the best markets for real estate investment at the local level to either flip properties or hold properties long-term as rentals. This book will teach you exactly how to fill that gap and reduce your risk; through a mix of institutional grade experience, master's level education and entrepreneurial grit, I will walk you through the entire process from start to finish.

Additionally, this book will take the market analysis to the next level and help translate information from the market analysis to help you compare deals. Meaning, this book will provide pricing strategies to ensure you maximize profits in the short and long-term and never overpay for properties.

Whether your business plan focuses on fix and flips or long-term rental housing, this book will help you uncover the best neighborhoods to invest within, while supplying a framework to reduce risk and maximize your profitability on any investment.

Background

Some might skim past this section quickly—you want to get straight to the good stuff! But I also think it is important to know who I am and where I am coming from.

In 2005, the fix and flip boom was going strong, and it seemed everybody I knew was getting in on the action. I did not have much capital to get started, but I *did* have strong financial and market analysis skills. I started to run proformas (financial underwriting models) and investment analysis for individual smaller investors. They were buying into anything from single family homes, to duplexes and one guy was working on 20–25-unit multifamily buildings. It turns out I had a knack for these investments.

My early success in these endeavors taught me that I wanted to go back to school and really understand what it meant to get into real estate acquisitions and development at the commercial level. So while I kept working, I went back to school part time to get my masters in real estate and construction management at the University of Denver. Here is where I started to put all my skill sets together and started to find my niche within the real estate industry.

I was a natural fit for the financial portion of the studies, but I also clued in on the market and feasibility analysis portions. I thought it fascinating to analyze markets from the national level down to the local competition. You have to be a bit of an economics geek to appreciate the idiosyncrasies and wanting to understand how the story all comes together for every investment. Understanding, there is a *story behind every investment*; the purpose of a market analysis is to understand the underlying story and use financial analysis skills to tell the story through proformas and other financial modeling. The key to any successful real estate investment, large or small, is being able to understand and communicate the story again and again.

When I graduated with my master's degree, it was August 2007; not the best timing for real estate. February of 2007 all REITs (Real Estate Investment Trusts) had taken a significant hit in the stock market on concerns of Chinese debt issues. September, warning of the debt levels in the US and massive mortgage banking issues were making headlines. October of 2007 the stock market peaked, and by June of 2008, the bear market declared itself losing 13% since October.

Luckily for me, I just slipped into the commercial real estate industry in February of 2008 as one of four new revenue managers for a major multifamily REIT. At the time, revenue management was a brand new discipline in the multifamily world—having proved itself as a mainstream practice since the 80s and 90s in airlines, car rentals, and eventually hotels. Multifamily was just starting to get into the practice, and I was one of the few on the forefront trying to make it work for our company.

If you're not familiar with revenue management, it is essentially the practice of optimizing revenue by aligning the right product with the right price at the right time for every customer. Think in terms of hotel stays. When you book a hotel six months out, the price is likely less than if you book the day of your stay. This is because the revenue management system is trying to optimize the revenue—which is a balance of occupancy and rate per room—for that hotel for that one night. When you book six months out, you are just starting to fill the hotel, so they are willing to charge a little less. By the time it is the day of your stay, they may only have 1–2 more rooms and they realize you probably *must* have that room that night. Therefore, they increase the price because they know your demand elasticity is extremely low and you will likely be willing to pay an exorbitant amount to stay there.

Demand elasticity is an economics term referring to how sensitive demand is relative to price.

We have all been "victims" of revenue management at some point. It is virtually impossible to avoid the practice as its benefits have permeated almost every industry. I even helped institute the philosophy with my fundraising charity. As we get closer to our events, we always raise prices!

In the multifamily industry, the practice is slightly different than it is in the hotels, or the airlines, or the car rental industry. You see, all of those industries have the ability to sell their inventory hundreds of times in a year. Hotels literally sell their rooms every night of the year. They could conceivably have a transaction/sale of a single room every day of the year—granted, hotels run at 70–75% occupancy and the average hotel stay is 1.5 nights depending on the location, but it is possible. This is a huge advantage when it comes to revenue management software as it gives extensive data for the revenue management algorithms/software to make very solid decisions to forecast future demand based on historical data.

Multifamily does not have this advantage. When we sell a unit, it is locked up for an average of 12 months; we only get to sell a unit once a year. A 300-unit multifamily building running at a stabilized 95% occupancy might sell 145 units to brand new customers and renew 140 customers throughout an entire year—285 transactions/observations. A 150-room hotel running at 75% occupancy might sell their rooms 27,253 times in a year!

The point is, as we were developing the practice of revenue management for our company, we realized we needed to supplement the lack of "observations" with heavy market analysis.

Throughout my career, I priced over 50,000 multifamily units across the country and have done market analysis from Southern California up the coast all the way to Seattle and across the country up and down the east coast from Boston and Manhattan to Philly, DC, Atlanta, and Miami. On top of my operational background, I've also helped underwrite over $1B in development and acquisitions. Since moving over to the development side of the business where I work today, I have actually worked on the redevelopment and ground-up development of over $150M in costs of multifamily projects.

However, every aspect of my professional career has come down to understanding how to analyze markets and extract the greatest amount of financial value from them.

From my local investment perspective, since getting involved in 2005, I've done a number of fix and flips myself and with partners, but I choose to mainly focus on rental properties which I started to get involved with back in 2009 at the bottom of the market in my area. Dealing with tenants is always an interesting game, but keeping the good ones comes down to service and price.

This combined local and institutional experience makes me uniquely qualified to write this book. Typically, most institutional professionals have no idea how to bring the breadth of market analysis tools they understand and apply it towards single family homes or smaller apartment buildings. The tools they use are just different. However, most local real estate investors do not understand the extent of options out there to analyze markets and be more specific with their market analysis or their presentation and understanding of the financials. As someone who has put these practices into use on both ends of the Institutional and local investor spectrum and been successful, I can translate the benefit of those experiences and creates a concise and repeatable process to help you succeed in analyzing markets and valuing properties.

This book will make you a better more informed investor.

Overview of the Book

"Every person who invests in well-selected real estate in a growing section of a prosperous community adopts the surest and safest method of becoming independent, for real estate is the basis of wealth." – Theodore Roosevelt

Neighborhoods Uncovered consists of 10 chapters walking you through a step-by-step process of evaluating markets starting at the broadest perspective and funneling down to ultimately individual properties. It is all about equipping you with the knowledge and confidence to make the best decisions based on a sound fundamental, professional, and disciplined investment approach.

Chapter 1: *Introduction to Market Analysis.* Starts with a general overview of what market analysis is and provides a mental framework to guide you through the journey, as well as the fundamental economic thought process behind the practice of analyzing markets.

Chapter 2: *Step 1 of the Market Analysis – Getting Started at the Highest Level.* Walks you through the beginning stage of the market analysis at the national level; teaching you what economic trends are most important to look for from a real estate investment perspective.

Chapter 3: *State Analysis.* This chapter takes you into the next level helping you establish property valuation and economic benchmarks within each state so you can create a basis for evaluation of trends at the county, zip code, and ultimately neighborhood level.

Chapter 4: *County Evaluation.* Here you learn residential demand shifts more to a focus on population or more specifically household growth than employment growth; exploring how to compare counties at a more detailed level and understanding what is most important to focus on, providing specific examples to illustrate the process.

Chapter 5: *Defining Sub-Markets:* Discusses defining specific geographical boundaries of your ideal markets and narrows in on the process for evaluating current housing supply and demand as well as a process for projecting those trends forward. This is where we also focus more on defining your target customer, so we can "cast the biggest net" ensuring your product appeals to the greatest number of potential consumers.

Chapter 6: *Neighborhood Analysis:* This chapter in many ways gets you to the epicenter of this book by illustrating how to uncover the best neighborhoods for you to invest within. It discusses the critical shift in your thinking that must take place to understand the demand for housing is no longer focused on easily quantifiable data as in the stages above, but rather is now heavily weighted on more qualitative "desirability characteristics."

Chapter 7: *The Market Based Approach to Analyzing Deals:* Here we take the findings from the work you did in the market analysis chapters above and begin to apply it to identifying and evaluating properties. I will cover how to evaluate specific property advantages and disadvantages and how to value each of those within your chosen market.

Chapter 8: *Proforma Financial Modeling and Setting up for Performance:* This chapter takes you through how to financially underwrite your deals for the expected life of the investment. This goes beyond the snapshot modeling of a single year back of the envelope calculation and teaches you professional investment underwriting skills used at the institutional investment level, helping mitigate risks and setting yourself up for success.

Chapter 9: *Pricing for Re-Sale, Pricing for Rentals:* This chapter walks you through the final step in the process of actually selling your property. This includes pricing the property from a rental perspective as well providing a framework for evaluating whether you should raise rents or not and by how much based on your specific market conditions; taking into account the risks of vacancy loss so you can make a confident, informed decision.

Chapter 10: *Summary:* As the title suggests, we bring the book to a close and wrap-up a summary of the teachings through concise bulleted takeaways and provide a resource for you to reach out for additional questions.

In addition to each of these chapters, at the end of the book, I include a number of Supply and Demand economic links providing additional resources for you to dig even further into the market analysis as questions come up specific to your markets or properties.

1

Introduction to Market Analysis

"Perseverance is not a long race; it is many short races one after the other."
– Walter Elliot

When I first started out in market analysis in 2005, I remember a time when one of the investors I was working with asked me to find data to backup why this was a great market. At that time nobody gave me a process or even a framework of how to do the analysis. I struggled with mounds of data and trying to decipher what was important with what was not. I can remember very specifically sitting in front of the computer going through national databases such as the Bureau of Labor and Statistics and the US Census information, chasing one rabbit down a whole after another. I wasted so much time, but at the end of it, I found facts on the market I thought most relevant. When I gave them to the investor, he said: "but this isn't what I want it to say..."

While it is questionable if I did the analysis correctly at the time, I could tell at least that it didn't matter. All he cared about was making the data justify why he was right and why the deal works in his mind. It is a common pitfall amongst investors to try and force the data to tell you why you're right. However, this analysis is not about manipulating your story to make the investment work. That process is fraught with risk and folly leading to bad investments. Market analysis should be about tailoring an investment around the story. That is often not a quick path, but one that takes perseverance to vet out the facts and do the work necessary.

The ultimate purpose of this book is to teach you how to analyze markets so you can buy your investment property correctly and price your product appropriately delivering on your financial expectations. We will run through examples which can be used for deals not yet purchased and for normal operations once you own the property. Keeping a pulse on the market is what will help optimize your investment returns.

I will post this diagram a few times throughout this book, but it is the basic filter of how you should think about analyzing markets.

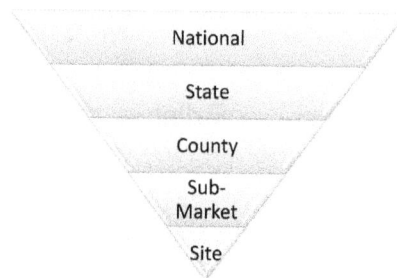

The shape of the diagram is important as it is meant to represent a funnel. Market analysis starts from the broadest perspective and narrows its way down to the most specific site. Each level refines the target a little more helping you decide where to invest based on the risk and returns. We will visit each one of these levels in this book, and I will guide you through free resources most relevant to local investors.

At the institutional level, we utilize all the categories since we can invest in properties across the country and in other countries. When I was working on my master's degree, I took a second job working for a financial institution helping to put together an investment thesis for a fund to invest in European REITs. We focused very heavily on the National part of this funnel as the political impacts could make or break any investment. At that point, we were so far removed from the assets themselves; it was better to invest in REITs on each stock market as they were far more liquid than obviously investing in the properties directly. If a leader was overthrown or the entire political system crashed, we could sell the paper and walk away.

For local investment purposes, it is good to know what is happening nationally and politically, to identify if there are any pending tax impacts or other legislation being proposed and how the national economy is doing with unemployment and GDP growth. On a day-to-day basis though, the national analysis will not likely change the way you look at investing in real estate. That being said, this will provide you with the framework to step out of the country if you so choose. Buying vacation properties in Mexico or Costa Rico could be a lot of fun as well, but admittedly, I have never analyzed those opportunities...

The next fundamental to understanding market analysis is one of the most basic economic theories, the law of supply and demand. This is the backbone to all economics and real estate investing is no exception. Effectively, as demand outpaces supply, prices increase. As supply outpaces demand, prices decrease. A market in an equilibrium state between demand and supply allows for measured or opportunistic price increases.

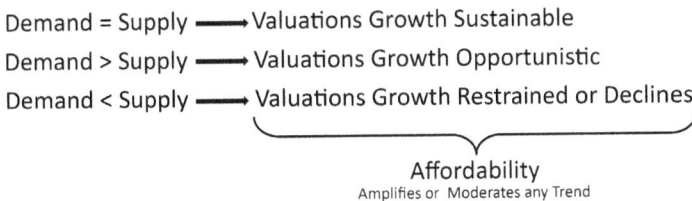

Demand = Supply ⟶ Valuations Growth Sustainable
Demand > Supply ⟶ Valuations Growth Opportunistic
Demand < Supply ⟶ Valuations Growth Restrained or Declines

Affordability
Amplifies or Moderates any Trend

The other factor that relates to that law is affordability. While it does not change the law itself, it does either amplify or constrain any trend. What this means is if demand is outpacing supply you should be able to raise prices. However, if people cannot afford the increase, it will lessen demand and return you back to an equilibrium or into an oversupplied situation. In real estate, an example of this equates to charging too much for the house you are trying to sell compared to the market. While your initial assessment suggested you should be able to get that price/valuation, if interest rates increase on mortgages there will be fewer people able to afford the price you think your house is worth. Thus, it sits on the market longer, or you end up reducing the price.

This theory layers in on top of the market analysis funnel at each level as we identify the demand and supply drivers. However, the part that trips up most people on market analysis is the understanding that the drivers of demand change as you move down the funnel and narrow in on specific neighborhoods. This, in my opinion, is the number one reason why so many people have such a hard time identifying the best neighborhoods to invest in. They continually try to force the same drivers at the national level down into the neighborhood level which is akin to forcing a round peg into a square hole.

At each level of this market analysis, we will walk through the *residential demand* drivers, so you understand how these are changing and can adjust tactics as necessary. These are different from office demand, which is different from industrial demand, which is different from retail real estate demand etc. So it is important to understand this book is focused on residential demand which works at the single-family home option for fix and flips up to multi-family rentals and everywhere in between on the residential real estate scope.

Since I touched on interest rates, I will elaborate a bit more as this is one question I get from friends and family regularly regarding national policies and the impacts of rising interest rates on property valuations. While a full analysis of this topic is outside of the scope of this book I will touch on the topic as it is timely in the current environment I am writing this book in.

What I would say: overall interest rates have an *indirect* correlation to real estate values. As interest rates rise they affect the ability of banks to borrow money and thus the cost of loans for real estate will increase. However, depending on the level you're playing at, this may not mean much if buyers only work in all cash. At the institutional level, we are not allowed to model debt into our underwriting as the deal must work on an all-cash basis. If we choose to add debt later on that should only be accretive to the overall deal.

As you work through the local level, the single unit rental properties, small office or retail properties are generally heavily encumbered with debt. Therefore, to sell the property, the buyer will likely need to take out debt. This makes the increase in interest rates far more impactful as affordability comes into play.

For example, if a property rents at $2,000/month, has expenses of $450/month before debt then you're all cash profitability is $1,550/month. However, once you encumber the property with debt and take out a loan of often 70–80% LTV (loan to value ratio), it can easily cost you $1,400/month depleting your profit down to only $150. If in that example your loan was at 3.5% and you go to sell the property the following year with the same rent and other expenses, but the interest rates have gone to 4.5% the monthly payment could easily jump $200! At that point, without knowing the market and how much to push your rents, you're rental will cost a landlord $50/month. Not exactly a prime investment any longer...

This book can add serious value to your investment and help protect you! I will help you optimize your rent levels or home prices and come up with an investment story to sell to any buyer. Think, if a buyer is looking at two properties and wants either your property or the one down the street, same sub-market and location advantage, but you can prove out a higher monthly rent. Instantly you have more value and can charge a higher price! This is another way to hedge your investment so even in a downturn or a rising interest rate environment you can deliver on your financial commitments.

If you're playing around at the 8–25-unit multifamily level or Class B office space or neighborhood strip mall, it is my experience investors are a mixed bag of heavy debt buyers, attempting seller financing or all cash. Every seller would always prefer all cash for the certainty and minimizing the risk of the deal.

At this level interest rates may or may not be impactful. Either way, if you can prove out a better monthly cash flow through higher monthly rents, you will still do better than the property down the street—no matter how the payment is structured.

Another key to market analysis is to always focus on the trends. An un-trended number by itself at one point in time will never tell the whole story. Watching a series of numbers each month, each quarter or each year will give you a much better idea of where things are going and what will come next.

Finally, it's important to understand market analysis is a journey, not a quick fix. It does take time to gather all the information and formulate a clear story. This is where self-discipline comes through; which in many ways, self-discipline is what separates the successful from the unsuccessful investor. This book is formulated to guide you through that journey and give you an edge on your competitors.

Summary

1. Market analysis is all about starting at the broadest perspective and narrowing down the funnel to the optimal site per your risk and return tolerance.
2. The law of Supply and Demand reigns supreme.
3. Affordability will constrain or enhance any trend.
4. Interest rates have an *indirect* correlation to real estate values.
5. Market analysis and rental rate increases are a way to hedge your investment.
6. Always focus on the trends.
7. Market analysis is a journey, not a quick fix.

2

Step 1 of the Market Analysis—Starting at the Highest Level

"The journey of a thousand miles begins with one step." – Lao Tzu

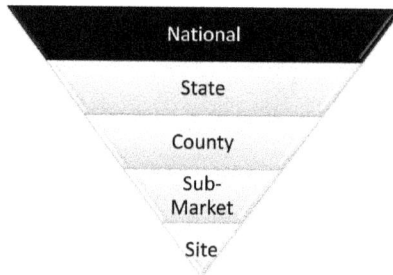

At the national level, there is no shortage of data or articles/opinions on future trends. This can actually be detrimental at times as there are so many opinions and many can be contradictive. It is best to find one or two sources you trust and stick with those whether you like the predictions or not.

To help find those sources, I am going to give a number of recommen- dations of websites to visit for information and data pulls throughout this book. It is important to know I am not getting paid for any of these suggestions. They are simply free resources that have proved out their value to me through my own market analysis experience.

One such resource is the Trading Economics.com website. They offer a free economic indicator section consolidating opinions of the "experts" and turning those into a consensus recommendation. You can find this resource with specific national economic commentary at https://tradingeconomics.com

I also like to use the "Livingston Survey" which is run by the Federal Reserve Bank of Philadelphia and summarizes the forecasts of economists from industry, government, banking, and academia. They usually only put out a white paper twice a year which is about how often I would look to renew this national section of the market survey.

I frequently take exerts of their written commentary and use that in the survey as you can see in my example report at the end of this chapter. Note of caution, it is fine to do that as long as you don't actually publish this market analysis online or elsewhere without giving them full credit.

Finally, if you simply want data tables with numbers to draw your own conclusions from, I would go with the Wells Fargo monthly economic forecast here: https://www.wellsfargo.com/com/insights/economics/monthly-outlook . It is a free resource that if you click on the "Economic Forecast" on the right side of the page, gives you a straightforward table to easily cut and paste into a report. It tells you far more than anything you truly need to know at the national level, but it does include the list below of the most important data points as well.

At this level, residential demand is focused on employment and broad economic indicators, so whichever source you utilize, the main points you're looking for are trends in:
  • GDP (Gross Domestic Product)

- Inflation (CPI)
- Interest Rates (Federal Funds Rate)
- 10-year Treasury Rate
- Employment/Unemployment

As you read through the information, you should be looking to identify the trends of each category and asking yourself the same question: "is the trend forecasted to go up or down and what does that mean for my investment(s)?" Notice, inflation and interest rates are analyzed to understand any affordability constraints looming on the horizon.

GDP

The importance of the Gross Domestic Product is to give an overall picture of the state of the economy. It represents the total dollar value of all goods and services produced over a specific period. As I am not an official economist I am going to borrow a loose explanation of why GDP is important to understand from Investopedia.com and their article "The GDP and its Importance" where they state:

"They [Nobel laureate Paul A. Samuelson and economist William Nordhaus] liken the ability of GDP to give an overall picture of the state of the economy to that of a satellite in space that can survey the weather across an entire continent. GDP enables policymakers and central banks to judge whether the economy is contracting or expanding, whether it needs a boost or restraint, and if a threat such as a recession or inflation looms on the horizon.

The national income and product accounts (NIPA), which form the basis for measuring GDP, allow policymakers, economists and business to analyze the impact of such variables as monetary and fiscal policy, economic shocks such as a spike in oil price, as well as tax and spending plans, on the overall economy and on specific components of it. Along with better-informed policies and institutions, national accounts have contributed to a significant reduction in the severity of business cycles since the end of World War II."

For purposes of this market analysis, the overall number is less important than the trend of GDP and the general opinions on the state of the economy. Effectively, an uptrend suggests the economy is strengthening, and a downtrend suggests a declining economy. If you are deciding to buy a property, it is important to understand renter or owner sentiment and if you are possibly buying at the top of the economy or at the bottom. If you already own your property, understanding the popular sentiment can help you identify if you should be raising rents or selling prices aggressively, moderately or not at all.

Inflation

Regarding inflation trends, real estate is a great inflation hedge because even in long-term fixed commercial leases of 3–10 years, there is always a place for inflation (often referred to as Consumer Price Index [CPI]) adjustment each year. This automatically means you do not lose value with a devaluing currency (inflation, by definition, weakens the purchasing value of currency). In multifamily or single unit residential properties you do not get to write inflation into the lease, but it should play into a part of your minimum increase each year. With the understanding, if you increase rents less than forecasted or actual CPI rate, you are technically devaluing the asset. That being said, a months' worth of no rent (aka vacancy loss) is far, far more negatively impactful so don't get too caught up in the minutia!

Additionally, even if the rents are not increasing proportionately to CPI, the property is likely still appreciating. As inflation grows, so to will the value of your overall property most likely which still creates the hedge to inflation.

Interest Rates

With interest rate trends, you're usually going to be most concerned with the federal funds rate and the 10-year note rate. The banks loan out mortgages based on a premium to the fed funds rate for a 30-year amortizing loan. If however, you're going towards a more creative structure such as short-term interest only or non-fixed rate debt than you'll be more interested in the 3-month LIBOR rate or prime rate—it really just depends on the product you're buying and the bank you're using as to which they prefer to base their premium against.

The 10-year note rate I mentioned above is important to keep an eye on from a financial returns perspective for your investors. If you're keeping this small and it is just your property or just a friends and family investment than this will be less important. However, the 10-year rate is the main rate sophisticated investors look at when they compare risk in an investment. The thesis being, they could invest in what is considered the safest asset class in the world and get likely 2.5% return (in the past 12 years has not gone above 3.5% and averaged roughly closer to 2.5%), or they can invest with you. If they invest with you, they should get a premium to this rate as they are taking on more risk.

In my experience with sophisticated real estate investors, if they could invest in the 10-year note at roughly 2.5%, they generally look for a minimum 6% to invest in REITs on the stock market (3% dividends and 3% stock price appreciation expectations at a minimum). Sometimes they can get up to 7–8% on preferred stock shares. Major Real Estate Operating Companies (REOCs)—which are mainly just large real estate companies not listed on the stock market and are thus far less liquid—they usually want 8–10%. For local investors, I usually see and hear about investors asking for 12–14% on the standard deal side. Some are getting more aggressive and also asking for 2–5% of profits on top of the 12–14% if you are flipping houses.

This has to weigh on your decision of whom to get involved in the deal and who not to involve in the deal. At least this gives some idea as to why they are asking for whatever they are asking for. If they are asking for less or more, it helps you evaluate if it is a good deal in comparison.

Employment and Job Growth

The final indicator to look for the trend at this level is employment and job growth. When jobs are growing, generally the economy is better off, and you will be more likely to raise rental rates or for sale prices. If jobs are contracting nationally, you will want far more details on this topic at the lower levels of the market analysis funnel to understand if this national trend directly impacts your markets.

Bottom line, whichever way the trend is headed, dig into this further in later chapters to understand how to capitalize or protect yourself, but at this level, you're more just trying to understand general customer sentiment.

There is a lot more to analyze on each of these topics, and you could write entire books on each one. However, for the purposes here, a quick paragraph on each and telling you were to copy and paste a table such as the Wall Street Journal, Livingston Survey and Wells Fargo Economics, will usually do nicely for the local investor.

Throughout this book, I'm going to include working examples of a market analysis and deal evaluation I recently completed. Adjust the examples as you need to in order to fit your specific analysis and projects. My goal was to provide a specific path, so you spend less time guessing and are more efficient in this process.

Below is an exert from the national section of my market analysis report. All of the charts and most of the commentary aside from the summary at the front are very simple to copy and paste from the links provided. Yet everything is summarized efficiently with everything you need to know about this topic for the immediate future and our purposes here. Each section has a 1yr graph and a 5yr graph both with trend lines (black) to help illustrate where each category has been going based on the historical data. This trend data line will not necessarily line up with the LivingstonSurvey commentary, but will provide a good counterpoint to check what they are saying vs. how things have been trending.

National Trends:

Summary: GDP is expected to increase into 2019 though moderating slightly from previous expectations and unemployment is expected to condense further by the end of the year and for the foreseeable future. Inflation is on the decline moderating to 2.3% for 2019 while interest rates and the 10yr note are both headed upwards. With the 10yr rate expected to hit 3.51% by the end of 2019 which could easily push 30yr mortgages close to 6%. As a result, we could see a stall-out in the market place to sell houses in 2019 as seller expectations may not match buyer's affordability.

GDP:https://tradingeconomics.com/united-states/gdp-growth-annual

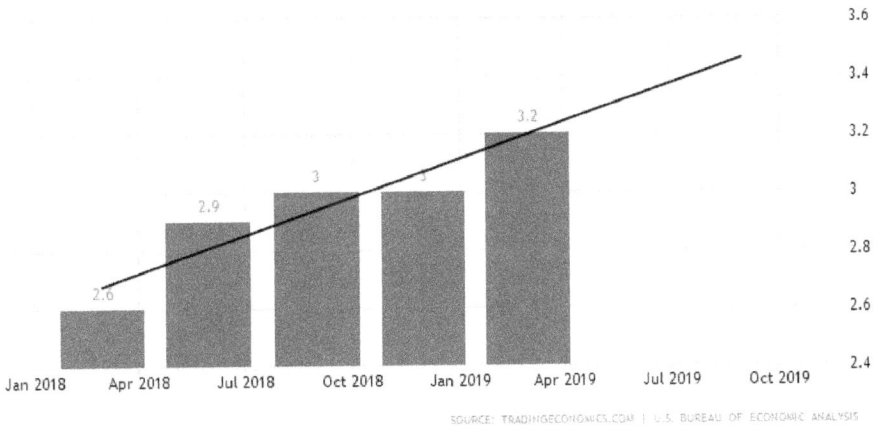

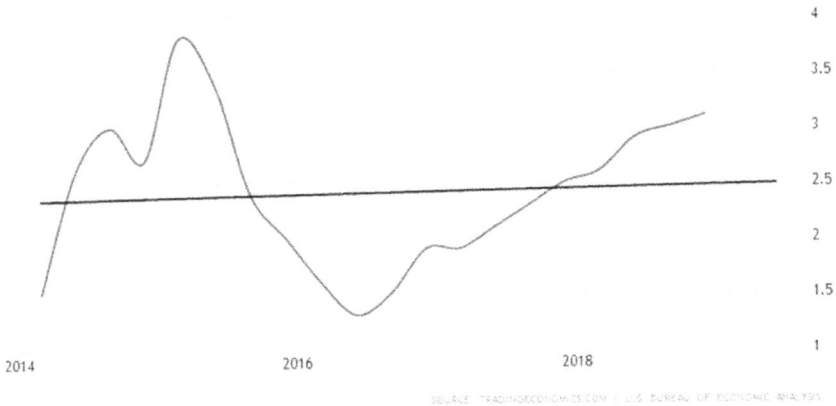

Livingston Survey Commentary: (https://www.phil.frb.org/research-and-data/real-time-center/livingston-survey/)

"*The forecasters, who are surveyed by the Federal Reserve Bank of Philadelphia twice a year, project that real GDP will grow at an annual rate of 3.0 percent in the second half of 2018. They see growth of 2.4 percent (annual rate) in the first half of 2019 and 2.3 percent (annual rate) in the second half of 2019. Compared with the June survey, these projections mark downward revisions for the second half of 2018 and first half of 2019."*

Employment https://tradingeconomics.com/united-states/unemployment-rate

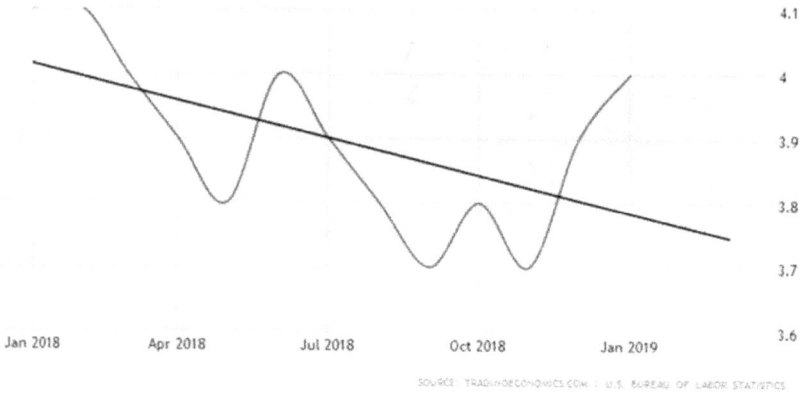

SOURCE: TRADINGECONOMICS.COM | U.S. BUREAU OF LABOR STATISTICS

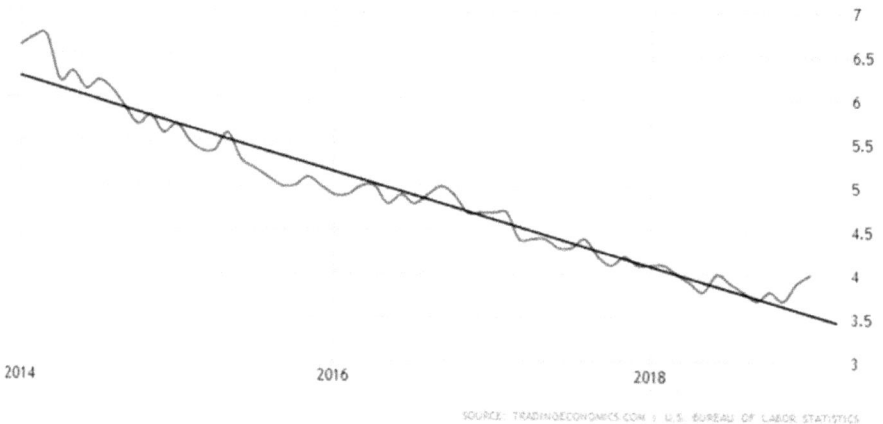

SOURCE: TRADINGECONOMICS.COM | U.S. BUREAU OF LABOR STATISTICS

Livingston Survey Commentary: *(https://www.phil.frb.org/research-and-data/real-time-center/livingston-survey/)*

"*The forecasters peg the unemployment rate in December 2018 at 3.7 percent (note that the forecasts were submitted before the December 7, 2018, employment report). The unemployment rate is predicted to be 3.5 percent in June 2019 and to remain steady at 3.5 percent in December 2019.*"

Interest Rates https://tradingeconomics.com/united-states/interest-rate

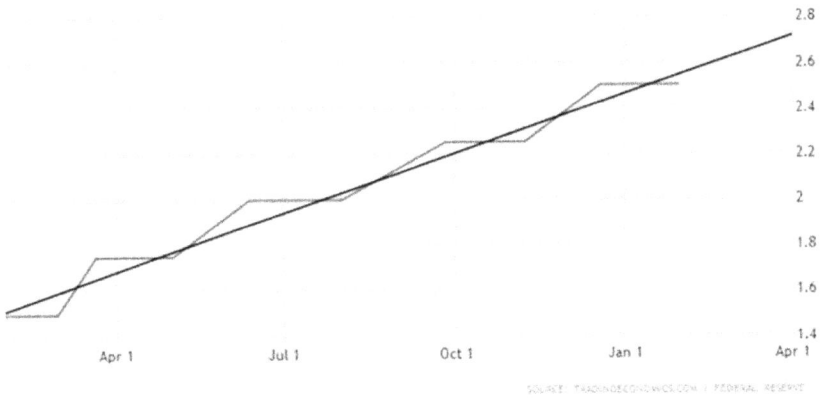

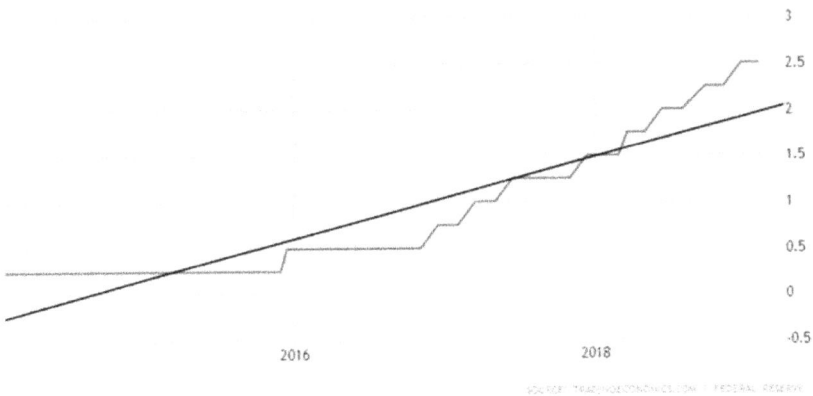

10yr Treasury Rates https://tradingeconomics.com/united-states/
government-bond-yield

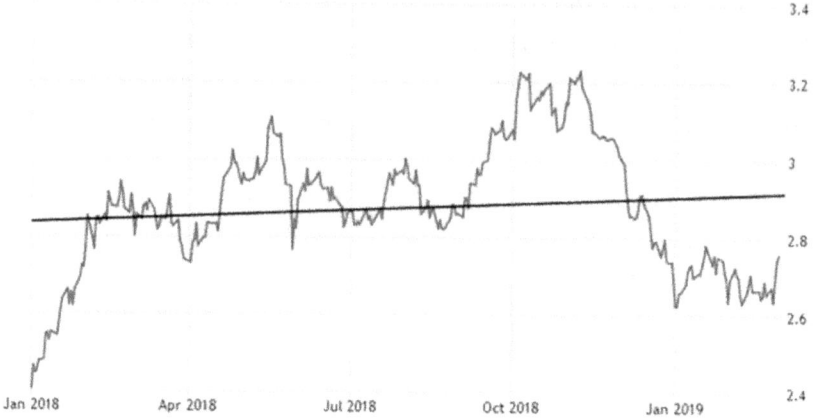

Livingston Survey Commentary: *(https://www.phil.frb.org/research-and-data/real-time-center/livingston-survey/)*

"Stronger Outlook for Short-Term Rates but Weaker Outlook for Long-Term Rates

At the end of December 2018, the interest rate on three-month Treasury bills is predicted to be 2.45 percent. The forecasters predict that the three-month Treasury bill rate will be 2.80 percent at the end of June 2019 and 3.01 percent in December 2019. The rate is expected to be 3.00 percent in 2020. The interest rate on 10-year Treasury bonds is predicted to be 3.20 percent at the end of December 2018, down from the previous estimate of 3.25 percent. Additionally, the forecasters predict the 10-year rate will be 3.42 percent at the end of June 2019 and 3.51 percent in December 2019. The forecasters expect the rate to be 3.55 percent in 2020."

Inflation: https://tradingeconomics.com/united-states/core-inflation-rate

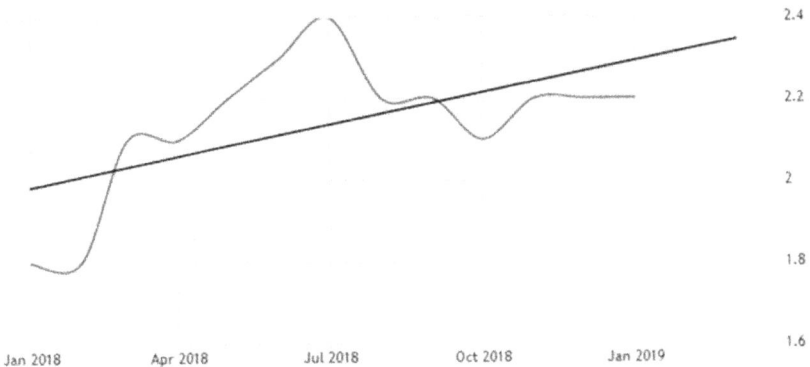

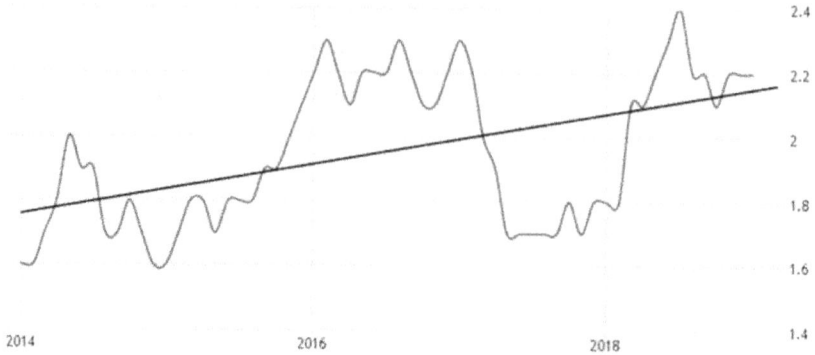

SOURCE: TRADINGECONOMICS.COM | U.S. BUREAU OF LABOR STATISTICS

Livingston Survey Commentary: *(https://www.phil.frb.org/research-and-data/real-time-center/livingston-survey/)*

"CPI Inflation Projections Hold Steady, While PPI Projections Strengthen On an annual-average over annual-average basis, CPI inflation is expected to be 2.5 percent in 2018 and 2.3 percent in 2019. The 2018 projection has been revised downward by 0.1 percentage point from that of the June survey, while the 2019 prediction remains unchanged. CPI inflation is expected to decrease slightly to 2.2 percent in 2020. PPI inflation is expected to be 3.2 percent in 2018 and 2.5 percent in 2019. The 2018 projection is 0.2 percentage point higher than the estimate from six months ago, while the 2019 projection is up 0.5 percentage point from six months ago. PPI inflation is expected to be 2.1 percent in 2020."

—-END of Market Survey—-

Summary

1. Residential Demand is defined by employment data and broad economic indicators at this level.
2. Affordability is understood through inflation and interest rate policies looming.
3. Your overarching goal in this section is to understand general trends and consumer sentiment.
4. GDP: the overall number is less significant than the trend of GDP and the general opinions on the state of the economy.
5. Inflation: increasing rents at the rate of CPI growth each year protects the value of your investment.
6. Interest rates: watch the fed funds rate to analyze where these are headed and at what rate banks will lend money. Understand the 10-year note and keep a pulse on the premium investors will require to invest in your project.
7. Employment: is the trend increasing or decreasing? Either way, dig into this further in later chapters to understand how to capitalize or protect yourself.

3

Step 2 - State Analysis

"Anytime you have population growth; there are business opportunities."
— Roland Dorson

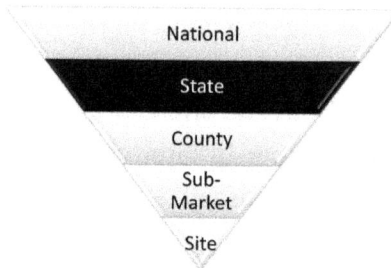

Local investing is always interesting, and the people you meet along the way keep it entertaining if nothing else. One such gentleman I have met was in an investing group I visited a few times, and he had no shortage of creativity, but he was one who lacked focus and would chase any shiny object. We ended up talking one night, and he brought up how he was headed to Mississippi next week to buy many houses and flip them for major profits. I simply asked what he knew about Mississippi that made these houses such a great deal. He said the housing is cheap and that he could get houses for less than $100K.

Me: *But what do you know about Mississippi?*

Him: *I don't know anything I've never been there.*

Me: *How do you know the $100K is a good deal?*

Him: *At $100k per house it is bound to be a good deal no matter what...*

I ran into this gentleman some months later and asked him how Mississippi was? He said it turns out all of the houses in this particular neighborhood needed to be re-built from the ground up. Additionally, he was told not to be on the streets past dark due to the amount of the crime and that people were leaving the neighborhood in droves; it was a complete waste of time.

This isn't to speak negatively about Mississippi; I think every state has this type of neighborhood somewhere. The point is that if he had done his homework, he could have saved himself the time and cost of going into an area like this.

————

This next level of the analysis helps you refine the information you learned at the national level and start digging deeper into those trends. The main key points you're going to look for here are:
- Home valuations
- Employment
- Population
- Wage growth

Residential demand at this level is focused on employment as well as population growth with affordability constraints identified through wage growth.

What you are looking for through each key point is to identify the states positively contributing the most to the national trends you just learned about. However, I'll be honest here, at the local level, if you live in Colorado and only have the option of flipping or renting properties in Colorado, learning all the coastal states are the best place to invest in won't help you. At the point where you aren't changing the state you invest within, it is most important to still do this part of the analysis and understand the key drivers of your state.

For instance, I live in Colorado. For years we have been known for the oil and gas industries as our number one industry. It still is even today, but the interesting trend has been the acceleration of the technology industry pushing through over the past 10+ years. This is important because if you believe this is a sustainable trend, you might choose to locate your investment property closer to heavy technology based sub-markets compared to oil and gas sub-markets.

The state level has its place in the analysis, but the truth is, at both the commercial and local level of real estate, you care more about the cities you're targeting. There also exists far more detailed information at the city and county level than exists at the state level; at the local level, you already have a general idea of what state you want/must invest in. I have only met one local investor in my time who was debating which state to invest in because his job had him splitting his time between two cities already. That being said, he was still more interested at the county level than he was at the state level.

I tell you these things, so you can be efficient in your time. These types of analysis can be cumbersome and if you are not used to doing them, very frustrating if you waste your time on metrics that won't likely change your strategy. My goal is to give you a re-creatable process you can update quickly and easily, even after you have purchased your property(s). To that end, I would not update this section more than twice a year.

I will say this once here at the beginning of the analysis and again in the summary at the end of the book, but as you work through each chapter, if you ever find the excel portion of the suggestions overwhelming, I have another resource for you. Just go to the website www.neighborhoodsuncovered.com and download the exact spreadsheet I have developed and used to refine this book. It has the exact same process within it and easy to follow steps to help you pull the data, but most importantly, a number of formulas to do the technical work for you. This will instantly give you a consistent approach to analyzing markets and underwriting individual deals while still being simple enough to encourage your self-discipline to repeatedly use this tool and maximize your investments.

Back to the analysis, the first screen to do at every level of the analysis from a residential business plan whether you are buying fix and flips or buying rental hold properties is to start by identifying the strongest home appreciation markets. For this, my favorite site to utilize is Zillow Data Research. I believe they do the best job out there as far as a free resource to consolidate and pull a lot of data together for you. Other sites such as Redfin do a good job as well, but their data is not as easy to work with coming in chart formats and cumbersome raw data tables. I like the flexibility of simple spreadsheet downloads, so I prefer the data tables of Zillow.

Home Valuations

Follow this link and go to the Zillow Data Research center https://www.zillow.com/research/data/. There is a ton of great data to work with here, but this is my attempt at helping you to narrow it down and not get lost in the weeds. Start with the Home Values section, under Data Type choose "Zillow Home Value Index (ZHVI) Summary (Current Month)" and under Geography, choose "State." Download the data and up will come a great spreadsheet listing every state and their associated home value appreciation percentages and average home values. The spreadsheet opens without any formatting so I would take a second and turn all the decimal numbers into percentages and turn columns including "ZHVI" into $ amounts; this just helps to clean up the picture.

Here I'll introduce a concept using the data to help you analyze the trends. People are always asking me how I find the hottest markets. This analysis will help you identify where those are by breaking down the analysis into three categories: Short-Term Markets (ST), Long-Term Markets (LT) and Stable Markets (Stable). Here is my general definition of the best of each:

- Short-Term Markets = "Hottest Markets" Where the MoM (Month-over-Month) and QoQ (Quarter-over-Quarter) average growth rates are the highest.
- Long-Term Markets = Where the 5-year and 10-year average growth rates are the highest.
- Stable Markets = Where the YoY, 5-year and 10-year average growth rates are all at relatively the same level.

When I started out at the local level, all I cared about were the hottest markets. However, at the institutional level with a longer-term buy and hold mentality, we are more concerned with stability and long-term average sustainability of the growth trends. There is less risk in the latter, but if your model is to simply flip houses, I would absolutely focus on the short-term hottest markets. Rental properties, I want the longer-term/stable markets.

When you pull open the spreadsheet, I would do a few things to identify each of these markets:

1. Update the formatting to percentages and dollar values as noted.
2. Off to the far right set up a few formulas to help identify the stages of each market:

Short-Term Markets: take the MoM values x 12 for every state to create an "Annualized" rate (A.MoM). Note: there is significant seasonality in the real estate business so do not just use this rate in your underwriting for monthly growth. This is a directional indicator only to compare to the YoY (Year-over-Year) rate.

- Then do the same thing for the QoQ values multiplying x 4 to arrive at an "Annualized" rate (A.QoQ).
- To identify the best ST market, set up a third formula to average the two together for each market. (A.MoM + A.QoQ)/2

Long-Term Markets: Simply set up a formula averaging the 5-year and 10-year growth rates for each market. (5-year + 10-year)/2

Stable Markets: Set up a final formula to average the 5-year, 10-year and YoY growth rates for each market. (YoY + 5-year + 10-year)/3

Some will debate this method, but I have found it repeatedly identifies all the three types of markets the easiest and most consistently.

Once you've set up those formulas, I would add one more to rank all the states [=rank(number,ref)]. This will allow you to identify where each state ranks within each category quickly. Again, at this level of the analysis, you are probably more interested in just where your state ranks and whether it is considered more of an ST, LT or stable market – defined by how high it ranks in each of the three categories. This analysis will add more value as we narrow down the analysis to counties, zip codes, and eventually neighborhoods.

Business Plans

Now is the time where your specific business plan and real estate investing objective starts to determine how you analyze the data. For purposes of this book we will narrow it down into two broad terms for the plans; either rental housing or fix and flipping houses. For myself, I have a spreadsheet that once I have determined my entire market analysis, and I'm simply analyzing deals, I always look at both scenarios for any property that comes across my desk. The amount of work it takes to analyze both scenarios vs. one or the other is a matter of 5 or 10 minutes once you have everything dialed in. Like I said above, the real difference between the two scenarios from a purely analytical perspective, is the intent and questions you should ask, depending on your track.

Fix and Flips

If you are heading down this road, in general, you are likely very interested in the short-term home value appreciation. Depending on the size of your property and level of finishes a flip could take three months or over a year. In general, most financing options I know about outside of cash are generally best to pay back in the 9 to 12-month range from closing.

Rental Analysis

If you're more into the long-term buy and hold mentality than I believe there is a different way to utilize the home valuation data. There are always varying opinions on how to analyze this data, but from my perspective, I consider real estate a long-term hold given its relative ill-liquidity compared to the stock market and other financial instruments. As such, I'm looking for consistently strong markets over time, and so I focus on the long-term markets and stable markets first.

However, even with a long-term mentality, you want to understand where the recent trend is headed. The YoY column will help illuminate this fact, and you want to see this number at or above the 5-year average. If Its less than the 5-year, but above the 10-year, it suggests the market is going to revert closer to its 10-year average—that may not be a bad thing. However, it could also be a sign the market is on its way into a decline; this might require waiting a few months and pulling this data each month to see where the trend is headed as the data is produced on a rolling basis each month. This means if you pull the data in August, the last year it calculated for YoY comparisons was August to July of the past 12 months. If you pull the data again in September, the 12-month calculation will be from September to August of the past 12 months. This is very helpful as it allows you to understand changing trends quickly by simply pulling the data once a month for the next few months. If during each of those pulls, the YoY number gap to the 10-year average does not materially change downward, it suggests more of a balance back to the 10-year average rather than an all-out decline.

Here is a table which gives you a quick way to think about the markets and what their trends are indicating.

If A.MoM	>	A.QoQ	=	Increasing ST Market			
If A.MoM	<	A.QoQ	=	Slowing ST Market			
If A.MoM	=	A.QoQ	=	Stable ST Market			
If A.MoM	>	A.QoQ	&	A.QoQ	>	YoY	= Hot ST Market
If A.MoM	<	A.QoQ	&	A.QoQ	<	YoY	= Declining ST Market
If A.MoM	>	A.QoQ	&	A.QoQ	>	YoY	= Increasing ST Market
If A.MoM	<	A.QoQ	&	A.QoQ	<	YoY	= Slowing ST Market
If A.MoM	=	A.QoQ	&	A.QoQ	=	YoY	= Stable ST Market
If YoY	>	5Year	=	Strong LT Market			
If YoY	<	5Year	=	Moderately Increasing LT Market			
If YoY	=	5Year	=	Stable LT Market			
If YoY	>	5Year	&	5Year	>	10Year	= Hot LT Market
If YoY	<	5Year	&	5Year	<	10Year	= Declining LT Market
If YoY	=	5Year	&	5Year	>	10Year	= Increasing LT Market
If YoY	=	5Year	&	5Year	<	10Year	= Slowing LT Market
If YoY	=	5Year	&	5Year	=	10Year	= LTable LT Market

Please note; I have very purposefully NOT provided all the possible outcomes of scenarios. The reason being, the table would take up two plus pages in the book and would take forever to interpret anyways. This table accommodates the basic scenarios I think most people will care about. More importantly, it teaches you how to think about the analysis so you can draw your own conclusions about those scenarios not presented.

This approach will allow you to choose the best markets from a home value and price appreciation standpoint. However, this part of the analysis needs to be complemented by actual economic data to substantiate the price movements and understand the broader picture of why. The next section breaks down the key economic factors to look for and provides free resources in each to help make it easier for you to find the information.

Employment Growth

At the national level, you wanted to look at overall employment trends to see if the state is adding jobs or losing jobs. At the state level we still want to know overall job growth trends. However it's more beneficial to understand which industries are growing fastest. Here we examine specific industries to understand which industry is the largest in the state and which is growing the fastest. You should watch out for this relationship. Often the fastest growing industry is the smallest, so the percentage change is large because it is on a small base. However, compared to the largest category, its relative size in the state may not be driving material job growth. The next few levels of city/sub-market and site level analysis will help you identify how much emphasis to put on each industry and which trend matters more.

As far as free resources to go to for this part of the analysis, I would suggest pulling up the Bureau of Labor Statistics (BLS) website: https://www.bls.gov/web/laus/statewide_otm_oty_change.htm. This will take you to a table highlighting all states and their relative employment growth year-over-year (YoY). You can sort this table by the highest growth percentage and see the top growing state. Remember it is all relative though, as of the time of this report Idaho was the top growing state, and North Dakota had declining employment YoY. However, if you live in Florida, as a local investor, Idaho is probably not an option for you to invest in and you probably don't know a lot about it. In real estate investing you are always trying to mitigate risks. A market analysis helps you understand the riskiness of an investment, but nothing replaces your local knowledge and understanding of the markets; I would not run off to invest in Idaho if I had never even been there before and had no way of sustaining any operations out there because I lived in Florida...

Additionally, a general overarching trend in understanding employ-ment growth is helpful, but it's often more helpful to recognize the specific industries growing. For that information, I would go to this link: https://data.bls.gov/cew/apps/data_views/data_views.htm#tab=Tables. There is a lot of data here so I would suggest choosing option 6 on the left-hand side of the page labeled: "High-Level industries, one area" »Then to the right, choose your year and state you are interested in evaluating (to speed things along I would type in the state in the "Search Area" below the list) » then press "Get Table."

The table is organized based on industry categories arranged by the NAICS (North American Industry Classification System) code. The NAICS is the standard used by Federal statistical agencies in classifying business establishments to collect, analyze, and publish statistical data related to the U.S. business economy—according to the Census.gov website. This categorization will help you stay consistent as we analyze the data at each level.

The key to understanding the data is that the first line of data "10 Total, all industries" is the sum of the second and third lines labeled "102 Service-providing" and "101 Goods-producing" NOT the entire table. Further complicating, "101 Goods-producing" is the sum of all the categories below it starting with the numbers 101; such as "**1011** Natural resources and mining." "102 Service-providing" is the sum of all the categories below it starting with the numbers 102; such as "**1022** Information." I've tried to illustrate this in the proceeding table to help you better understand the data.

Industry	Quarterly Establishments	Month1 Employment	Month2 Employment	Month3 Employment	Total Quarterly Wages	Average Weekly Wage	Month3 Employment Location Quotient	Total Quarterly Wages Location Quotient
10 Total, all industries	170,267	2,455,971	2,509,049	2,540,248	$34,787,777,417	$1,070	1.02	1.02
102 Service-providing	141,844	2,002,533	2,035,391	2,051,630	27,288,353,440	1,034	1	1.01
101 Goods-producing	28,423	453,438	473,658	488,618	7,499,423,977	1,222	1.11	1.09
101 Goods-producing	28,423	453,438	473,658	488,618	7,499,423,977	1,222	1.11	1.09
1011 Natural resources and mining	3,091	26,079	28,767	29,129	335,667,568	922	0.71	0.6
1012 Construction	16,581	109,128	124,630	134,218	1,949,866,490	1,223	0.91	0.89
1013 Manufacturing	8,751	318,231	320,261	325,271	5,213,889,919	1,248	1.29	1.25
102 Service-providing	141,844	2,002,533	2,035,391	2,051,630	27,288,353,440	1,034	1	1.01
1021 Trade, transportation, and utilities	37,644	525,354	533,848	534,741	6,315,774,752	914	0.98	1
1022 Information	3,974	49,149	49,184	49,510	917,800,056	1,433	0.88	0.61
1023 Financial activities	16,062	176,981	177,484	179,512	3,721,313,956	1,608	1.1	1.1
1024 Professional and business services	32,186	374,662	378,366	380,060	7,592,693,126	1,546	0.91	1.03
1025 Education and health services	19,162	524,360	527,188	527,122	6,505,744,387	951	1.18	1.16
1026 Leisure and hospitality	15,477	263,474	279,828	289,301	1,487,290,737	412	0.87	0.77
1027 Other services	17,339	88,553	89,493	91,384	747,736,426	640	1.01	0.88

Once you understand how things are organized, you can focus on all the categories EXCLUDING the Total, Goods, and Services. Since those are just the summation of all other categories, they will always be the largest but aren't that helpful. It is important to know if your state is more a goods-producing state or a service-providing state. However, even once you know that, you care more about what type of goods and services are being produced.

Rank the 10 or 11 remaining industries based on their size of total employment. I would then pull this table two more times for the past two preceding years and compare the growth rates each year of those industries. This will help you put together the story to understand which industries are the most significant based on size and growth. The important thing to understand here is what are the top 3–5 industries and are they growing or declining based on the trends in the table. How do those trends compare to the national average? Start thinking about where in your state these industries are concentrated? "People of a feather tend to flock together" so if healthcare is significant in your state where are the hospitals located? Hospitals tend to act as a hub for other medical offices and medical resources. To support those areas they need housing nearby for workers and the customers of those facilities, retail to support a lifestyle, and office space to support the professionals both directly and indirectly affiliated with the industry.

Population Growth

The next important metric at this level is population growth. States often go through trends of migration and emigration (people coming into the state and people leaving the state). The link here is a great place to pull data from https://www.census.gov/data/tables/time-series/demo/popest/2010s-state-total.html - Again, sometimes these links can be difficult. If this link does not work, I suggest Googling: "State Population Totals: 2010-2018." The listing you need is usually in the top three of the non-paid advertisements with the same heading.

I would pull the first excel table there labeled: "Annual estimates of the resident population for the United States..." If you identify the growth YoY for the past three years than average those, you can use that average as a projected growth for the next two to three years. This is a top-line number, but it will suffice for the detail needed at this level on any of the subjects. Again, staying top-line, the only trend you're really looking for here is positive vs. negative growth. The relative strength can be important, but again at the local level, you are not likely to change which state you invest in based on this data.

However, if you are in a declining population state, I would dig into more articles as to why it is declining? Why are people leaving? Where are they going? What industries are most affected? Ultimately, this will have the greatest impact at the county and sub-market level. As you drill down, there are often counties or sub-markets still growing and far outpacing the state level trend. As we move into those parts of the analysis, we will vet this out further and identify resources to help get the answers to those questions.

Wage Growth

This is important to understand as the more income people make, the higher rents or housing prices they can afford. There are a few cities where real estate rents and valuations can far outpace wage growth and do just fine such as Manhattan, San Francisco, etc. However, this is not a sustainable model for most markets. Each of those markets is uniquely positioned based on the strength of employment, supply constraints and overall desirability. The less risky formula for real estate investing for everywhere else is to identify markets where wage growth is in-line or outpacing rental rate or home valuation growth.

A great place to start is by going to this site: https://www.bls.gov/sae/#tables at the BLS. This one is a bit ugly to pull so stay with me. When you click the link, just pull the last spreadsheet (XLS) link under: "XXXX Annual Average Tables," then choose: "Average hours and earnings of all employees on private nonfarm payrolls by state." Once the spreadsheet is downloaded, you can easily evaluate by state the past three annual "Average Weekly Earnings" growth trends.

Once you have your wage growth data, compare the home valuation data you pulled from Zillow. Then ask the question as to whether or not wage growth is outpacing home valuations? If it is, great, if it isn't you will want to dig into this more. If the imbalance is due to more demand for housing than currently supplied, it could be a great opportunity.

The more economics centric people believe when doing this type of analysis, it is important to also note inflation at the state level as an affordability constraint. I would suggest that it is not really necessary. The reason being, understanding overall inflation is growing at 1.5 to

3.0% is not going to change how or if you invest in a property. The classic economic example is to examine the impact of inflation on a gallon of milk. If the milk goes from $1.99 + 3% (which would be aggressive inflation growth), the price goes to $2.05; not likely to change your investment strategy on real estate. I get the point; it is the cumulative effect on all products that do begin to impact affordability concerns. However, the U.S. city average since 1990 has had average annual inflation growth of 2.4% per year. So for the impact of inflation to influence your investment theory, it would have to be significantly above the average. In my milk example above, the *aggressive* 3% growth is only 0.6% above the average which really only increases the gallon of milk roughly one penny. I think I will still invest in real estate with that impact.

Inflation does hold some value at the national level which we discussed in the previous chapter as you should keep a tab on it and understand the general sentiment and direction. Again, at that level, you were trying to stay broad and understand the general market sentiment of the consumer. Often times news headlines can be more impactful on the consumer psyche than the actual financial impact itself.

The important aspect to remember along with all of these categories you are analyzing is to understand how they compare to the national average. You pulled the national average on the previous section, so I would merely put a note next to each table. If your chosen state is growing faster or slower than the national average than asking if that is a good or bad thing as it relates to your business plan. Understanding, even declining markets can create great investment opportunities!

The other aspect you care about on each of these subjects is their forecast. The truth at this level is most forecasting companies/websites will simply take the past few observations and forecast the trend forward. Even many of the paid resources essentially are doing this same methodology which you can do yourself pretty easily. If we go back to the population example just above, the link I gave you turns out a table with a 7-year history. If you identify the growth YoY for the past three years than average those, you can use that average growth as a projection for the next two to three years. As mentioned previously this is a top-line number, but it will suffice for the detail needed at this level on any of the subjects.

Below is an exert from my Market Analysis report I created for the state portion of the summary and Employment sub-section. While at the national level we used charts from Trading Economics.com, the tables shown here are self-made, but don't get too intimidated or bogged down with creating your own. Remember, at the end of this book I have a link to a spreadsheet walking you through each section of this analysis with the same tables already set up.

State Trends:

Summary: At this point in the analysis two states are rising to the top of my opportunity list with both Colorado and Nevada. Colorado has a stronger long-term trend and stability in home valuations, but Nevada has better economic factors. However, they are both the number one and two positions of each category. As such, I am going to review both in the county section next to see which has the best opportunity in the local markets.

Home Value appreciation trends:

Of my top 5 states, ONLY New Mexico is seeing a short-term price appreciation (Mississippi is #1 in the country). However, THE top state in the country from the 10yr growth perspective and number 3 in the country for 5year growth is Colorado. While the state is in a Short-term projected "softening" of the market, long-term, it looks to have staying power.

State	A.MoM	A.QoQ	YoY	5Year	10Year	Ave. Home $	LT Mrkt	Values
National Ave.	-1.1%	2.0%	6.5%	6.2%	1.8%	$216,700		
Minnesota	-2.1%	-1.1%	5.2%	6.5%	2.0%	$225,100	4	4.1%
Colorado	**-0.7%**	**0.2%**	**6.3%**	**9.5%**	**5.1%**	**$364,600**	1	7.3%
California	-0.2%	0.9%	6.1%	7.4%	3.2%	$539,400	3	5.3%
New Mexico	0.0%	3.5%	6.9%	3.9%	0.2%	$186,600	5	
Nevada	-1.3%	3.4%	11.2%	10.6%	2.2%	$275,200	2	

Economic Analysis:

Of my top 5 states, Nevada ranks number 1, outpacing all the other states listed with clear upside on their wage growth. This could add serious legs to their home valuations. However, Colorado came in number two here on the economic factors which mean the two states just flip-flopped and are both interesting at this point in the valuation.

Weighting		50%	30%	20%				
State	Employment	Population (3yr Projected)	Wage Growth (3yr Projected)	Rank	Top 5 Growth Industry		2yr Ave. Annual Growth	Weighted Score
Minnesota	1.1%	2.4%	1.7%	4	1025 Education and health services		2.7%	
Colorado	2.8%	4.4%	3.4%	2	1012 Construction		5.8%	
California	1.6%	1.4%	2.5%	3	1025 Education and health services		3.3%	
Nevada	**2.8%**	**5.9%**	**5.1%**	**1**	**1012 Construction**		**8.9%**	
New Mexico	1.5%	0.2%	-0.2%	5	1012 Construction		5.3%	
National Ave.	1.6%	2.0%	10.7%					

—-END of Market Survey—-

Summary

1. Residential demand at this level focuses on overall employment growth and industry-specific growth as well as population growth
2. Affordability constraints are identifiable through wage growth
3. The state analysis is important to include as it will identify general trends you need to be aware of, but even if you aren't debating between states, focus on understanding the trends and forecasts.
4. The key indicators to evaluate and compare to the national averages are:

-   Home valuation trends and if your state is a "hot" market with greater short- term appreciation trends and/or a great long-term or stable market.
-   Employment growth rates
-   Unemployment rates
-   Top industries
-   Population growth and Immigration and emigration trends
-   Wage growth outpacing or lagging against home valuations?

4

Step 3 - County Evaluation

"True genius resides in the capacity for evaluation of uncertain, hazardous, and conflicting information." – Winston Churchill

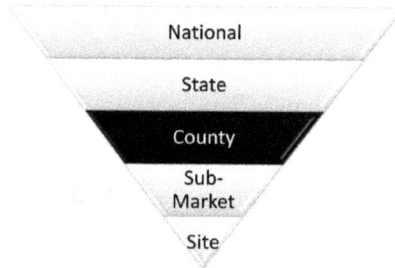

Deciding between markets is rarely a clear cut story. Often there are markets that will excel in one portion of the analysis and fall flat on others. The evaluation of one from the other must be done based on priorities weighing in what is more important to you and the investment.

While you probably weren't debating between which countries to invest in or likely which states, you could choose between counties and cities. The issue here is depending on which county or city you are analyzing, those may be two separate areas, or they could be the same; the determining factor is usually the density of population within those areas. At this level of the analysis, you could also easily throw in the complication of pulling data at the MSA (Metropolitan Statistical Area). However, for the purposes of this analysis, I have made a sincere effort to keep it simple and stay at the county level rather than seep into the MSA or city level. *The important factor is to stay consistent.* However, you decide to analyze at this level, just stay consistent, or the data will not end up painting a clear picture, and you can easily get confused by the results.

At this level of the analysis, the residential demand is based more on the population growth than employment growth. Understanding it isn't that employment is not significant, but from a residential perspective, you do not have to live in the same county as you work in. As such, the major driver shifts to household formations which is the number one driver of housing in any market. You also no longer look at inflation as the affordability issue here, but wage growth at the household median income level is the most important to identify affordability for rent or mortgage payments.

Home Valuations

Here we need to utilize the Zillow home valuation data again to help us screen for stronger home valuation markets. As you did previously, start with the Home Values section.

Home Values » Data Type » ZHVI Summary (Current Month) » Geography » County

Just as you did for the state section previously, when you pull open the spreadsheet, I would do a few things to identify each of these markets:
1. Update the formatting to percentages and dollar values as noted.
2. Off to the far right set up a few formulas to help identify the stages of each market:

Short-Term Markets: take the MoM values x 12 for every state to create an "Annualized" rate (A.MoM). Note: there is significant seasonality in the real estate business so do not just use this rate in your underwriting for monthly growth. This is a directional indicator only to compare to the YoY (Year-over-Year) rate.

- Then do the same thing for the QoQ values multiplying x 4 to arrive at an "Annualized" rate (A.QoQ).
- To identify the best ST market, set up a third formula to average the two together for each market. (A.MoM + A.QoQ)/2

Long-Term Markets: Simply set up a formula averaging the 5-year and 10-year growth rates for each market. (5-year + 10-year)/2

Stable Markets: Set up a final formula to average the 5-year, 10-year and YoY growth rates for each market. (YoY + 5-year + 10-year)/3

Once you've set up those formulas, I would add one more to rank all the counties [=rank(number,ref)]. This will allow you to quickly identify where each county ranks and allow you to choose your top 3-5 to examine closer as we dive into the economics section.

The next qualifier I would look for is the actual home value itself. As of the time I'm writing this book if I simply look at the top performing Short-Term market in the country in terms of appreciation, the data would suggest I invest in Santa Clara County, CA. The issue, the average home value is $1.3M—just a bit outside my range today...

If you're a local investor in the same boat, it is important for you to understand this fact as part of your investment story. To the same point, the lowest average home values within the top 30 zip codes for appreciation, have home values at $102,071; far more interesting from my affordability perspective. However, there is also a note of common sense here to manage. A market with extremely low home values generally has low values for a reason...

This is where, again, this market study will pay dividends if you have the discipline to finish the market analysis and truly develop your story around why you would invest in this market. It may very well be, this market is going through a re-gentrification renaissance of sorts and is poised to skyrocket. If so, run with it, get in there and double down. If that is not necessarily identifiable, I would caution heavily. A low-cost market will generally produce low selling prices and low rents. Both put pressure on your margins not leaving much room financially for any unexpected costs or vacancy - both of which WILL HAPPEN so buyer-beware...

Rental Values

This brings us to the next level of the Zillow analysis. Scroll halfway down the page of the Zillow Data research and look for Data Type.

Data Type » ZRI Summary: Multifamily, SFR, Condo/Co-Op (Current Month)

"ZRI" stands for Zillow Rent Index and "SFR" stands for Sing Family Rental.

The spreadsheet produced essentially summarizes and averages all rental listings for all residential product types. At this level of analysis, I would not dive into the debate about which product type is doing better and which you should invest in as a result: multifamily vs. SFR (Single Family Rentals) vs. Condos. The critical part here is purely understanding the market average rental rate is trending up and identifying which markets are doing the best.

Here again, filter all the columns, sorting the YoY column from highest to lowest. You'll note quickly this does not provide a 5-year and a 10-year history. This makes the data less clear as to a trend the first time you pull it, but it is great to pull this once a month and start cataloging your own trends as you analyze deals; more than likely you will hopefully be at this longer than a month.

For these purposes, I would do two things with this data next. First, I would compare the YoY rental value increases to the home values analysis. Are the fastest rising rents in the same markets with the fastest rising Home Values? Second, the best angle I think to analyze the YoY data is to average up all the values for each market quickly. From there, any increase above the average is theoretically the stronger county.

The next part of this analysis is where the art comes in. Data can only take you so far and then at some point you have to start making decisions informed by the data you've pulled but may not tie in 100%. What I mean is at this point, you may have identified a great market to work in, but depending on your business model, this analysis may bring to light conflicting reports.

For instance, the market I most preferred based on the numbers and taking a buy and hold rental approach, does not have a clear winner in my example analysis. The largest rental rate increases YoY do not correspond to the best YoY, 5 or 10-year home valuation appreciation markets. At this point you should side with thinking long-term in my opinion—I am somewhat conservative. I would side with the markets having the greatest home value appreciation and average to above average rental rate growth. This helps to reduce risk as you have more data supporting the long-term appreciation trends of home values than you do on rental rate growth. If the rental market crashes for some reason, you should theoretically still be able to sell without losing your principal in the investment.

Additionally, the value of home appreciation on a percentage basis is a major multiplier in comparison to the same percentage growth in rental rate increases, i.e., a 3% growth on the valuation of a single family property year over year is much more impactful on value creation and investment returns than a 3% growth in rental rates year over year.

Employment/Wage Growth

Much like at the state level, we want to know how employment is trending at the county level. To stay consistent, it is worth using the BLS.gov website again to pull this data by following this link: https://data.bls.gov/cew/apps/data_views/data_views.htm#tab=Tables

Option 19 on the left-hand side » Select your market to the right, but keep the lower area list focused on "10 Total, all industries » Then press "Get Table." Again here you are looking for the latest YoY growth of employment in the area. Compare each county together to identify the fastest growing county.

An added benefit of using this resource is that it also pulls in the wage growth as well in the same data. You should use this YoY growth number as the basis for comparison vs. your home valuation growth to watch for affordability issues previously discussed.

The next step is to understand in which industry the growth is occurring at this county level and work through the top five industries. Again, you did this same process at the state level so to stay consistent follow this link: https://data.bls.gov/cew/apps/data_views/data_views.htm#tab=Tables.

Choose option 6 on the left-hand side » Select your market to the right»Then press "Get Table." When the data comes up, focus in on the top 10 –11 sectors outside of: Total industries, Goods-producing, and Services-producing we discussed in the state section. Pull this data for the current year and past two years focusing on identifying growth trends within the top five most significant industries for each county.

How does each industry sector compare to the overall county growth average? If your top sized industry is declining which sector is making gains? Is there a medium-sized industry driving the growth you could capitalize on? Using my healthcare/hospital analogy as before, "People of a feather tend to flock together" so if healthcare is big in your county where are the hospitals located? How can you capitalize on the growth!

An important note here, when we talk about investing in housing next to major employment centers, there are really two types of overarching themes in my opinion when it comes to housing. One, there are people who want to live close to their work. This is usually born from the necessity and pain of commute times. Think of Manhattan, most people who work in Manhattan want to live there because the commutes are a minimum one hour if you live outside the island and often times I've heard closer to two hours—one way! However, if you're buying an investment property in Idaho, commute times may not be a concern, sol living close to work may not be a major driver of demand.

The other theory is that people live where they want to wake up on Saturday morning. This thought is born from the idea people want to unplug from where they work. They want to be able to relax and keep work at work and live on the weekends and nights spending time with family and friends.

This type of person, by the way, isn't precluded from living in the city or near CBD's. Generally, if they are a younger person with no kids, the city may very well be where they want to work and wake up on a Saturday morning because they want to be in the middle of the life of the city. The focus of this mentality though should be locating a place where people can relax. This may be a far-reaching suburban neighborhood with great schools or next to a major neighborhood retail location.

The critical aspect is to use the data we develop here to come up with a reason why you are investing where you are and who your target customer is.

Why do people want to live where you are investing? What is going to keep them there? Understanding those drivers is what is going to allow you to be able to flip the house for the most profits or raise rents consistently and reduce vacancy maximizing your investment returns.

Population Growth

As in the last two levels, you are still looking for a general trend of population growth. However, at this level, we also want to start going more in-depth and identify the growth of Household Formations (HHF). Household Formations represent anything from a single person needing a studio apartment to a family of eight needing a 5-bedroom house to two roommates buying a 2-bedroom condo and everything in between. Every "formation" effectively just means there is one more statistical unit of demand for housing. That is why it is more important than population growth on its own which includes children and elderly not able to live on their own. What we care about, is what drives up the demand for housing.

The best free resource for both types of population information is again going to be the census.gov website located at this link: https://factfinder.census.gov/faces/nav/jsf/pages/index.xhtml#. It works at the county level so just type in the counties you are evaluating (one at a time). As always, you're looking for trends, so under the population category select the "XXXX [year] Population Estimates Program"; I would simply paste the information for your three to five counties on a spreadsheet and evaluate the growth from the first year to the most recent year.

While the data is good, the critical part, is understanding the trend. I always add on a trend to the right of the data for the next three years, merely averaging the growth from the prior three years and forecasting that forward—the same method as used previously. It's not perfect, but for this analysis, it works great to help directionally projects the trend. See example here:

Population Growth Table

| Geography | 1-Apr-10 | | Population Estimate (as of July 1) | | | | | | | Frcst Annual | State Rank | Frcst 3yr |
	Census	Base	2015	2016	2017	2018	2019	2020	2021	Growth	Order	Growth
Denver County, Colorado	600,158	599,813	681,618	694,777	704,621	704,621	712,483	718,498	723,192	2.04%	9	2.6%
Arapahoe County, Colorado	572,003	572,174	628,834	636,949	643,052	643,052	647,872	651,560	654,424	1.37%	11	1.8%
Boulder County, Colorado	294,567	294,572	317,968	321,173	322,514	322,514	324,046	325,011	325,848	1.06%	14	1.0%
Weld County, Colorado	252,825	252,839	284,382	294,243	304,633	304,633	311,740	317,833	322,376	3.40%	6	5.8%
Adams County, Colorado	441,603	441,702	489,822	497,395	503,167	503,167	507,706	511,197	513,906	1.62%	10	2.1%

For household formations, use the same Census.gov link then choose:

Housing » "XXXX [year] Population Estimates Program"

Follow the same evaluation shown again here:

Household Formation Growth Table

| Geography | 1-Apr-10 | | Housing Unit Estimate (as of July 1) | | | | | | | Frcst Annual | State Rank | Frcst 3yr |
	Census	Base	2015	2016	2017	2018	2019	2020	2021	Growth	Order	Growth
Denver County, Colorado	285,797	285,635	305,558	313,657	320,545	320,545	325,724	329,862	333,035	2.25%	8	3.9%
Arapahoe County, Colorado	238,301	238,326	245,524	247,487	251,714	251,714	253,818	255,970	257,407	1.03%	15	2.3%
Boulder County, Colorado	127,071	127,073	132,738	134,092	135,920	135,920	137,000	137,985	138,681	1.12%	12	2.0%
Weld County, Colorado	96,281	96,286	103,761	106,848	109,869	109,869	111,994	113,772	115,107	2.87%	7	4.8%
Adams County, Colorado	163,136	163,156	169,069	170,542	173,120	173,120	174,495	175,836	176,752	1.11%	13	2.1%

Ideally, you want to choose the fastest growing county from a total population perspective as well as household formations. Remember, household formations drive housing demand more than straight population growth. If you pick three counties with all declining or flat population growth, focus on the county with the most significant household formation growth.

Renters vs. Homeowners

After population growth, you want to pull in additional data on renters vs. homeowners. Obviously, the more renters as a percentage of house-holds the better for the rental business plan, the more homeowners as a percentage of households the better for the fix and flip business plan. Remember, the actual numbers are far less impactful as the percentage growth trends. Knowing there are 140,000 renter-occupied apartments is helpful, but not nearly as impactful as the fact they grew 10% in five years compared to the other county you were evaluating which only grew 4%.

At the institutional level, we do care about the actual numbers as well as the percentage growth because in my job today I am usually going to be building and adding enough apartments into the market it will affect how the market reacts. My competition is doing the same thing, and at some point, you can oversaturate the market with too much supply and not enough demand. However, as a local investor, I am usually concerned only about one or two units on any given month rather than 30 plus units in any one neighborhood. Since my risk and exposure is so much less, I'm fine with just knowing the trends of the market rather than the specific counts of supply.

A good free-resource for this information is the "City-Data.com" web-site http://www.city-data.com . Type in each county you're evaluating separately. The "renter-occupied apartments" are generally located in the first few paragraphs with the latest date and a starting date from the census data; the difference between the two highlights your most recent growth.

Evaluation

At this point you've pulled the data for the 3–5 counties you were interested in and can see side-by-side which numbers are stronger than others. Sometimes you will end up with an obvious winner, but most of the time you will end up with a mix of data points not pointing to a clear winner. Evaluation at this point is what we refer to as the "art" of market analysis. It has been my experience in the past that it is worth ranking the indicators by their level of importance. This way if a market is healthy on the top three rankings and weaker on the lesser rankings, you can still make a good decision as to where to focus your investments. Remember, the critical part of each data set is the trended projection for the next two or three years.

Here is how I would rank the characteristics we just discussed in this chapter:
1. Household formations
2. Population growth
3. Employment growth overall
4. Wage growth/affordability comparisons
5. Employment growth in the top three industries

Below is an exert from my Market Analysis report again for the county section this time:

County Trends:

Summary: At the end of evaluating the top five counties in both states, I'm only going to pursue Colorado to the next level.

From a valuation perspective, Colorado has the stronger long-term market growth characteristics better adapting to my typical model of preferring to rent out properties. The top three Colorado counties all offer double-digit 5year appreciation and roughly 6% 10year appreciation opportunities.

From an economic perspective, Colorado won out here as well with the overall average for the top five counties greater than those of Nevada. Additionally, the household formations in Colorado are almost 2x those of Nevada on average with both Weld and Denver County coming in well above that average.

Adams County, however, is a solid number three county economically but with two better options in Denver and Weld County, I'm not planning on pursuing that market any further despite the healthy valuations.

Home Value appreciation trends:

As I compared the top five counties within both states, it was clear Colorado had a much better long-term average. This is not surprising given the housing crash and knowing Nevada was one of the hardest hit during that time. However, that very fact is suggestive of their volatility potential which leads me to side further with Colorado as the more conservative choice.

Within Colorado, the top three counties are all relatively tight on the long-term metrics, but on the shorter-term metrics, Denver County has a slight edge as the only county with a positive annualized month-over-month metric (A.MoM), suggesting they might be coming back on the up-swing of the cycle.

State Selected	County	A.MoM	A.QoQ	YoY	5Year	10Year	Ave. Home $	Rent Inc.	LT Mrkt	Values
Colorado	State Ave. -->	-0.7%	0.2%	6.3%	9.5%	5.1%	$364,600	0.3%		
	Adams	-0.7%	-0.1%	7.4%	11.7%	6.6%	$328,100	2.2%	1	9.1%
	Denver	0.9%	-1.0%	7.0%	10.9%	6.5%	$413,500	2.0%	2	8.7%
	Weld	-2.7%	1.2%	8.3%	11.0%	5.9%	$311,900	3.2%	3	8.5%
	Arapahoe	-1.6%	-1.8%	5.7%	10.1%	5.9%	$366,000	3.2%	4	6.0%
	Boulder	-0.9%	0.4%	4.8%	9.3%	5.3%	$522,500	1.2%	5	7.1%

State Selected	County	A.MoM	A.QoQ	YoY	5Year	10Year	Ave. Home $	Rent Inc.	LT Mrkt	Values
Nevada	State Ave. -->	-1.3%	3.4%	11.2%	10.6%	2.2%	$275,200	2.8%		
	Washoe	-2.7%	0.9%	8.4%	11.6%	3.2%	$350,200	4.9%	1	7.4%
	Carson City	0.8%	3.5%	8.6%	11.1%	2.1%	$290,300	4.8%	2	6.6%
	Clark	-0.5%	4.0%	12.0%	10.5%	2.0%	$263,300	2.3%	3	6.4%
	Lyon	-0.5%	1.6%	11.9%	11.6%	0.0%	$247,100	9.3%	4	5.8%
	Douglas	-2.2%	2.4%	6.4%	5.0%	2.8%	$165,800	-2.7%	5	3.5%

Economic Analysis:

Based on the summary economic analysis tables below the average of each of the top five counties for each state suggests Colorado has the strongest economic profile. While Nevada is not bad, the household formations of nearly double in Colorado are probably the best indicator of residential demand within a county in my opinion.

Within Colorado, the top two counties to really evaluate next are Weld County and Denver County of which Weld County is clearly very strong across the board. It's interesting to note their most aggressively growing top 5 industry is Natural resources and mining at 18.5% each year for the past two years. As I dig further into this county, I'm going to be looking to see if I can identify specific sub-markets and neighborhoods this might be impacting.

Weighting	35%	25%	20%	20%				
County	HH Formations Growth	Employment Growth	Population Growth	Wage Growth	Weighted Rank	Top 5 Growth Industry	2yr Ave. Annual Growth	Weighted Score
Average	3.0%	3.2%	2.7%	7.8%				
Denver	3.9%	2.3%	2.6%	6.5%	2	1026 Leisure and hospitality	3.1%	
Arapahoe	2.3%	2.3%	1.8%	5.7%	4	1026 Leisure and hospitality	4.6%	
Boulder	2.0%	1.9%	1.0%	6.8%	5	1013 Manufacturing	5.2%	
Weld	4.8%	6.0%	5.8%	12.5%	1	1011 Natural resources and mining	18.5%	
Adams	2.1%	3.4%	2.1%	7.4%	3	1021 Trade, transportation, and utilities	4.1%	

Weighting	35%	25%	20%	20%				
County	HH Formations Growth	Employment Growth	Population Growth	Wage Growth	Weighted Rank	Top 5 Growth Industry	2yr Ave. Annual Growth	Weighted Score
Average	2.8%	3.2%	4.3%	6.6%				
Washoe	4.7%	3.3%	5.3%	7.0%	1	1012 Construction	10.8%	
Carson City	1.1%	5.4%	1.4%	9.9%	4	1024 Professional and business services	5.6%	
Clark	3.9%	3.0%	6.7%	4.5%	2	1012 Construction	8.1%	
Lyon	2.5%	2.6%	5.8%	6.9%	3	1012 Construction	13.5%	
Douglas	1.8%	1.8%	2.1%	4.5%	5	1013 Manufacturing	5.2%	

—-END of Market Survey—-

Summary

1. Household formations are a more impactful force behind residential demand compared to straight population growth alone.
2. General employment growth is important, but keep watching the trend of the top 3–5 industries as you move down the analysis to find the industries driving the majority of the growth.
3. Wage growth is the prime indicator of affordability at this point.
4. Understanding the makeup of your market between renters vs. homeowners will be a key driver in identifying the business plan for you as you continue down the analysis.
5. Answer the following questions:

- What is happening with the overall population growth and more importantly household formation and Income level trends?
- What is happening with Jobs?
- What major industries are growing the fastest? Do you know where they are concentrated (think hospital analogy)?

5

Step 4 - Defining Sub-Markets

"Experience without theory is blind, but theory without experience is mere intellectual play."

— Immanuel Kant

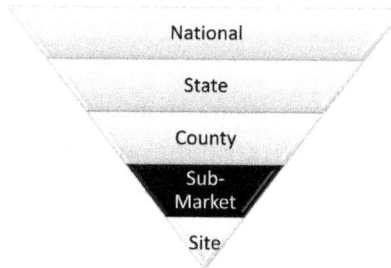

So often in this world, we look to think "outside of the box" and look for ways to expand doing things differently; there is value in that practice. However, in investing, having the discipline to stay within your sandbox is often times more beneficial. There is extreme value in becoming an expert in your field, tracking changes in a market over time, understanding every street in the neighborhood, every amenity the neighborhood has to offer. Experience does matter, but experience only happens over time. The best way to accelerate your experience is to focus on specific areas of expertise. In real estate investing, one avenue to do just that is to define your sub-markets clearly and learn everything you can about them. Then track those markets regularly so you can identify trends faster and truly know the value of any investment. This is one of the best ways to eliminate risk in any investment; there is no replacement for experience and living history.

At this point, we are going to assume you have chosen your county to dive into deeper. As mentioned before, depending on your market, the tricky part for this next level of analysis is in understanding (from a data perspective) certain cities can be equal to entire counties and apply to the previous chapter, or they can be small enough to be sub-markets and confuse you in this chapter.

There are two things to understand about the term "sub-markets." The first is the basic definition which suggests a sub-market is broadly defined as a distinct part of a larger market. In real estate, a market is typically a county, MSA or a large city and a sub-market is a smaller defined area within the market such as a smaller city, zip code or neighborhood.

The second point to understand is that ultimately at the local level a sub-market is whatever you define it as. This is why the first step when analyzing sub-markets is to delineate the boundaries clearly. At the commercial level, we usually have a REIS, Axio, CoStar, MPF or other third party companies define the sub-markets for us. However, that is confusing when comparing them to one another as the defined boundaries do not exactly match each other...

At the local level, my suggestion is to always start with analyzing zip codes then going down to the neighborhood level if possible. The reason being, zip code data is readily available from both free and paid resources and allows you to rank and justify the creation of your sub-market. They also rarely change and can easily be evaluated amongst multiple data sources equally. Note, not all zip codes have neighborhoods consistently defined so in some instances this may be the lowest level you can reach with broader data.

If you do have the neighborhood level of data, I would repeat this process below for both levels. The reason being is that you are always trying to identify trends and understand the full story. Simply going from the county level straight into the neighborhood level may be too much of a jump to understand what changed from one to the other. Each market has its nuances and differences so do whatever makes sense for you. If your story doesn't quite add up, you should always expand this analysis as extensively as you need to, to understand the why.

At the zip code level, residential demand focuses almost entirely on population and household formations. However, here we also start adding in supply of housing numbers to really begin to understand the supply and demand calculation which helps us to identify if there is more or less demand than supply; going back to the earlier lesson on economics.

Wage growth is still the number one factor of affordability here, but we continue to look more into the actual household income to understand what the specific average rent or mortgage levels are. From a rental perspective rents under $1,000 per month put significant stress on your margins when debt is included. We'll talk more about this at the deal evaluation levels, but it is something to keep in mind at this point so you can prioritize your time.

Home Valuations

You might be getting tired of going back to Zillow, but my goal is to be consistent and make this analysis less cumbersome. Sticking with an easy and repeatable data source is the best way to go here.

First, go to https://www.zillow.com/research/data/.

Home Values » Data Type » ZHVI Summary (Current Month) » Geography » Zip Code

Follow the same process you have already completed on the past two sections for setting up formatting and market indicator formulas indicating ST, LT, and Stable markets. This will allow you to quickly identify where each zip code ranks and allow you to choose your top 3–5 to examine closer as we dive into the zip code economics section. Note on this one, when you pull the spreadsheet, if you don't first filter down to just your primary counties and DELETE all other rows, the over 15,000 rows of data will bog down your spreadsheet analysis.

Rental Values

If you're focused on fix and flips you may think pulling the rental data here does not apply to you. I would suggest there still may some benefit to understanding your market and telling the story through this information. For instance, if you are in a high demand market where rental rates are skyrocketing; home ownership will be far more attractive. Especially, if you are going after the first time home buyer who is usually caught up in the rental game. If however, rental rates are moderate and just sticking around the national historical average of 3% per year, there is less incentive for people to get out of the renting game and buy that first house. It is up to you and what story you are trying to tell.

To find this analysis, go back to Zillow Data Research, scroll halfway down the page and under Data Type, pull "ZRI Summary: Multifamily, SFR, Condo/Co-Op (Current Month)."

Here again, filter all the columns, sorting the YoY column from highest to lowest. How are the YoY rental values increasing compared to the home valuation growth rates? Second, the best angle I think to analyze the YoY data is to average up all the values for each market quickly. From there, any increase above the average is again the stronger zip code.

Economics Section

Assuming you've filtered down to your top 3–5 zip codes based on the valuations and/or rental rate growth, it's time to get more into the details as we zero in on specific neighborhoods and sites to target. The data is less friendly to pull here as you cannot easily pull a quick spreadsheet as we have been doing, but it is worth it to be disciplined enough to put the full story together.

At this point, go back to the City-Data link: www.city-data.com and look up each of the zip codes individually. City-Data.com does a great job with data, but you can very easily get lost in the weeds with too much data. I would suggest focusing on finding the following data and thinking about each in terms of the questions below:

- **Population growth**: How does this compare to the county and state average? What can you forecast forward based on the numbers given? Which of your zip codes are growing the fastest?
- **Unemployment rate:** How does this compare to the county and state average?
- **Supply of existing housing units**: The sum of all of these types of housing will inform you as to the total supply of housing in the

market. We will utilize this later in the Demand and Supply section of this analysis.

- **List of top industries**: How do these compare to your state and county analysis? Are they the fast-growing industries or not?
- **Renter-occupied vs. Owner-occupied residences:** Speaks to your breadth of market whichever business model you are pursuing.
- **Average household size**: Will usually be around 2.5, but if it creeps closer to 3 or closer to 1.5, it could impact the size of the house, condo or townhouse you choose to purchase.
- **Average AGI (Adjusted Gross Income)**—*This is equivalent to the Wage growth we have been analyzing in previous chapters:* How much has it grown? What is that on an average annual growth? What is the projection of income growth over the next few years and which zip code is growing the fastest?
- **List of Neighborhoods within the zip code:** You'll use this for the next chapter on identifying the site you are competing within.

Demand and Supply

"I am like any other man. All I do is supply a demand." – Al Capone

At this level of the analysis, it is important to start cluing in on the supply of housing in your market as well as the relative demand for housing. As I noted, in the beginning, I have spent years working on market analysis and working to understand the demand elasticity for pricing of apartments across the country. No matter how great your product is if supply outpaces demand your price will come down. If demand outpaces supply your price will go up - basic economics. This simple concept holds very true throughout the real estate world. Unfortunately, getting this equation right in the heat of decision making is one of the most elusive tasks of any real estate professional.

However, once you have pulled all your economic data for each zip code, we can use formulas and assumptions to try and get closer to finding markets where demand is outpacing supply or will be soon...

- **Current Housing Demand:** Take the total annualized population projected for the current year and divide by the most recent total household formations. In my market analysis example at the end of this chapter, I used a projected 35,648 population for 2018 divided by 2.0 household formations to come up with a demand of 17,807 housing units.
- **Current Housing Supply:** This is merely the sum of all housing noted under "Housing Unit Structures." In my example, this is equal to 15,258.
- **Current Housing Shortfall/ (Oversupply):** Simply divide Current Housing Demand by Current Housing Supply and subtract one. 19,749/15,258 = (1.167 − 1) x 100 = 16.7% shortfall. A positive percentage means there is a shortfall of housing in the market giving you pricing power for your asset.

That process will give you a good idea of the current housing demand and supply picture. Projecting this number forward is really where the money is in terms of helping to identify if now is a good time to enter into the market. To attempt that feat, you follow this set of formulas:

- **Annual New Housing needed:** Take the annual growth of population divided by the household formations. In my same example the annual growth of population is 4,966/ 2.0 HHF = 2,483
- **Rental housing vs. Owner-occupied housing:** To understand how much of that new supply of housing should be renter vs. home ownership apply the percentages you pulled earlier and multiply by the Annual new housing needed. Example: 2,483 x 63% renters = 1,564 rental units needed.
- **Annual New homes being added:** Within citydata.com is a graph labeled "year house built." Within that graph is a point that will say "Built 20XX or Later." Take this number and divide by the

annual growth from the current year to that given year. Example: Built 2014 or Later = 56, if today is 2018, take 56/ 4 = 14 new housing units assumed to be added each year.

- **Shortfall/ (Oversupply):** Subtract Annual New homes being added from Annual New Housing needed. Example: 2,483 – 14 = 2,469 shortfall of homes
- **New Homes % Shortfall/ Oversupply:** Take the Shortfall/ (Oversupply) and divide by the Current Housing Supply to come up with a percentage shortfall or oversupply for each zip code. Example: 2,469 / 15,258 = 0.1618 x 100 = 16.2% shortfall of homes

The top two numbers you want to understand are the "Current Housing Shortfall/ (Oversupply) %" and the "New Homes Shortfall/ (Oversupply) %." These two numbers will be the most helpful when comparing to other zip codes (the larger the positive number, the better) recognizing the magnitude of opportunity in one zip code vs. another.

Understanding this is not a perfect process, but for the local investor, it will work just fine. Again, you are not adding hundreds of housing units to the market; most local investors are usually just looking for the impact of one or two. In an effort to keep this to free resources this is the best solution I have been able to devise, and it gets you close enough for local purposes. The most important aspect is to focus on the percentage growth when comparing the numbers amongst zip codes. The greater the positive percentage, the better your chances of staying in an appreciating market.

Once you've pulled all the data, I would score each category based on a weighted average as to which zip code had the best result in your opinion. My default weighting is:

1. 25% - Current Housing Shortfall/ (Oversupply)
2. 25% - New Homes % Shortfall/ (Oversupply)

3. 20% – Population Growth
4. 10% – Unemployment Rate
5. 10% – Average Adjusted Income growth
6. 10% – Household Affordability

As before, if there is a clear winner than this methodology is excellent, but if they are within a few points of each other, then you should go back to the art and go with your gut. This is where you probably already know a little about each zip code anecdotally. Ideally, I would take a drive out there and actually see for yourself what the type of neighborhoods look like and what your thoughts are for the opportunity to invest. This also helps to think about if you want to drive out to each zip code regularly. I have reviewed a few zip codes that looked good on paper, and then I drove out there and just decided I simply didn't want to work in those neighborhoods; that may be a conclusion which outweighs some of the data for you.

The other data points I suggested you pull above (but aren't ranking) are more to help you with the qualitative aspect of this analysis. This is where you start to put together the picture of the ideal buyer or renter based on the most significant opportunity.

Again, the numbers and this analysis will help guide you and give you a disciplined investment approach, but it will still always come down to your gut/the art of the deal to decide where you want to invest.

Below is an exert from my Market Analysis report again for the zip code section this time. Please note, if you have trouble seeing any of the table examples presented in this book, go to the website: www.neighbor-hoodsuncovered.com and download the pdf of the completed market analysis. There are a number of size restrictions I'm held to through online book publishing that we can get around with supplemental reports. It's also helpful to download so you have a complete reference to have when you go to put your own market analysis together.

Zip Code Trends:

Summary: My top zip codes to review further are 80247, 80223, 80239, and 80631. Each of the markets has healthy demand characteristics, very good long-term valuations, decent affordability and generally a higher propensity towards renting.

Home Value appreciation trends:

In both counties, the top seven zip codes are extremely strong from a long-term valuation perspective. However, the edge goes to Denver with the top four zip codes each ranking higher than the number one zip code in Weld County. Denver is, however, a bit sluggish on the rent growth, well below the national average above 3% currently. Weld County has a couple at 5.8% and 4.1% YoY that will keep me looking at them a little further in the economic section.

State/County	Zip Code	A.MoM	A.QoQ	YoY	5Year	10Year	Ave. Home $	Rent Inc.	Rank Rent	LT Mrkt	Values
Colorado	County Ave. -->	0.9%	-1.0%	7.0%	10.9%	6.5%	$413,500	2.0%			
Denver	80219	0.4%	0.1%	12.3%	16.5%	8.6%	$313,800	2.4%	1	1	
	80223	0.4%	-1.2%	8.5%	15.6%	8.3%	$326,800	2.3%	2	2	
	80204	-1.0%	-2.4%	9.2%	15.1%	8.5%	$369,600	2.0%	3	3	
	80247	2.1%	2.5%	11.5%	15.7%	7.8%	$229,700	1.6%	5	4	
	80239	-0.4%	-0.8%	7.1%	14.6%	7.9%	$295,100	0.1%	7	5	
	80205	-0.3%	-0.4%	7.7%	11.8%	7.9%	$455,500	1.9%	4	6	
	80207	1.1%	-1.3%	6.1%	11.9%	7.6%	$445,000	1.1%	6	7	

State/County	Zip Code	A.MoM	A.QoQ	YoY	5Year	10Year	Ave. Home $	Rent Inc.	Rank Rent	LT Mrkt	Values
Colorado	State Ave.	-1.0%	1.2%	6.8%	8.9%	4.1%	$216,000	1.6%			
Weld	80514	-0.4%	4.3%	9.7%	15.1%	8.1%	$292,900	1.3%	5	1	
	80621	-3.4%	0.8%	9.8%	15.4%	7.6%	$285,300	-0.7%	7	2	
	80631	-2.1%	3.5%	12.2%	14.1%	7.3%	$233,700	5.8%	1	3	
	80620	-3.7%	1.4%	10.9%	13.2%	7.1%	$262,000	4.1%	2	4	
	80530	-2.2%	1.9%	10.7%	12.2%	6.8%	$324,900	1.0%	6	5	
	80643	-1.5%	0.3%	10.0%	12.5%	6.1%	$319,200	3.5%	3	6	
	80645	-2.3%	3.6%	10.4%	12.0%	6.6%	$255,300	2.3%	4	7	

Economic Analysis:

Each county has some very interesting Demand and Supply characteristics making them both desirable in certain zip codes. However,
within Weld County, the only market I'm really interested in based on
this analysis is Greeley or 80631. While the unemployment number
jumps out at you first, understanding one of the top economic drivers
associated with this zip code is a major university; this could easily
offset both the unemployment rate as well as explain the in-balance
in housing demand. More digging is necessary to see if the shortage is
closer to the University and thus supporting my focus on that specific
sub-market area despite not having any designated neighborhoods.
This would also support the greater rent increases identified in the
valuations section.

All the other zip codes within Weld County are simply less desirable to
focus on today for one reason or another noted below.

- 80530 – This one has a number of good economic attributes but
  notice the housing demand numbers are extremely low. This is
  due to only having 4,500 people in the entire zip code which given
  its location, suggests it is rather rural in nature. This could be
  further assumed or corroborated based on the 83% owner occupied
  housing rate. I'm not interested in a rural model so despite being
  number two, this one will be ruled out.
- 80514 – Looks decent across the board except for the amount of
  new housing being added to the area. I would need to understand
  where and what type of housing is being added to see if there was
  an opportunity in this zip code.
- 80620 – Definitely nothing bad based on the numbers, but no wow
  factor either drawing me up there.
- 80621 – With zero population growth happening and an oversupplied housing market, there are just better opportunities to focus
  my time.

	Average	80514	80621	80631	80620	80530
City Name		Dacono	Fort Lupton	Greeley	Evans	Frederick
Population Growth	1.7%	2.8%	0.0%	2.1%	1.6%	2.2%
Unemployment Rate	4.6%	2.5%	4.1%	8.9%	4.2%	3.1%
Average AGI (Adjusted Gross Income)	2.8%	3.5%	3.1%	2.4%	2.3%	2.6%
Household Affordability	$1,336	$1,385	$1,495	$1,077	$1,156	$1,568

Demand vs. Supply Analysis based on Population Growth

Current Housing Demand	6,946	1,926	4,305	20,013	6,790	1,697
Current Housing Supply	6,540	1,815	4,509	18,051	6,674	1,653
Current Housing Shortfall/ (Oversupply)	3.4%	6.1%	-4.5%	10.9%	1.7%	2.7%
Annual New Housing Needed	122	54	(1)	415	107	38
Rental Housing	61	20	(0)	228	50	5
Owner Occupied Housing	62	33	(1)	187	57	32
Annual New Homes being Added	28	48	0	70	14	6
Shortfall/ (Oversupply)	95	6	(1)	344	93	32
New Homes % Shortfall/ Oversupply	1.1%	0.3%	0.0%	1.9%	1.4%	1.9%
Weighted Rank:		1	5	2	4	3

Demographic and Consumer Trends Information

Renter vs. Owner Residences %				Greatest % Renters		Greatest % Owners
Renters	37%	38%	30%	55%	47%	14%
Owners	63%	62%	70%	45%	53%	86%
Percentage of Family Households		Family Centric	Family Centric	Family Centric	Family Centric	Family Centric
Family Households	56%	57.0%	54.3%	49.9%	56.3%	60.0%
Nationality and Ethnic Majority						
White	56.9%	60.7%	50.2%	46.3%	51.8%	75.7%
Black	0.8%	0.5%	0.5%	2.0%	0.7%	0.4%
American Indian	0.4%	0.5%	0.5%	0.5%	0.5%	0.3%
Asian	1.2%	2.1%	0.9%	1.3%	0.8%	0.8%
Native Hawaiian and Other Pacific Islander	0.0%	0.0%	0.0%	0.1%	0.0%	0.0%
Other	0.2%	0.1%	0.1%	0.2%	0.3%	0.4%
Two or more races	1.3%	1.4%	1.0%	1.2%	1.2%	1.6%
Hispanic or Latino	39.1%	34.8%	46.7%	48.4%	44.8%	20.8%

Within Denver County, the 80247 zip code is the most interesting having solid population growth, decent affordability, and a very high supply shortage. The propensity to rent at 63% also aligns better with my preference for rental properties. Unfortunately, I was not able to ascertain specific zip codes impacted from the Natural resources and mining industry growth noted on the county analysis.

- 80239 – Also looks good from a demand characteristic, but the affordability is very low, and the higher ownership is less appealing.
- 80223 – Looks perfectly decent on the demand factors, slightly more renters and affordability is above $1,000 which is my preferred threshold.
- 80219 – The major issue here is affordability which is telling me this is a neighborhood I will not focus much time on given the likely thin margins.
- 80204 – Demand is slow here, but affordability is very good. However, the heavy current supply imbalance and lack of population growth will likely put pressure on the valuations. I will track this market, but not looking to get in today.

65

NEIGHBORHOODS UNCOVERED

	Average	80219	80223	80204	80247	80239	Weighting
City Name		Denver	Denver	Denver	Denver	Denver	
Population Growth	4.2%	1.9%	1.8%	0.7%	13.9%	2.5%	20%
Unemployment Rate	4.9%	4.5%	3.9%	6.9%	4.0%	5.1%	10%
Average AGI (Adjusted Gross Income)	1.9%	0.7%	2.0%	4.4%	1.9%	0.3%	10%
Household Affordability	$1,058	$804	$1,045	$1,405	$1,187	$849	10%

Demand vs. Supply Analysis based on Population Growth							
Current Housing Demand	15,018	21,883	7,796	12,859	19,749	12,803	
Current Housing Supply	13,992	21,399	7,597	13,863	15,258	11,845	
Current Housing Shortfall/ (Oversupply)	7.0%	2.3%	2.6%	-7.2%	29.4%	8.1%	25%
Annual New Housing Needed	743	417	142	87	2,753	315	
Rental Housing	442	204	77	58	1,735	136	
Owner Occupied Housing	301	213	65	29	1,019	180	
Annual New Homes being Added	32	0	40	107	11	0	
Shortfall/ (Oversupply)	711	417	102	(20)	2,742	315	
New Homes % Shortfall/ Oversupply	4.8%	1.9%	1.3%	-0.1%	18.0%	2.7%	25%
Weighted Rank:		3	3	5	1	2	
Weighted Score:		2.9	2.9	1.4	4.4	3.5	100%

Demographic and Consumer Trends Information						
Renter vs. Owner Residences %				Greatest % Renters		Greatest % Owners
Renters	55%	49%	54%	67%	63%	43%
Owners	45%	51%	46%	33%	37%	57%
Percentage of Family Households		Family Centric	Family Centric	Family Centric	Average Households	Family Centric
Family Households	47%	55.5%	41.9%	40.6%	33.5%	65.0%
Nationality and Ethnic Majority						
White	24.4%	21.4%	32.2%	31.1%		13.0%
Black	9.1%	1.2%	3.0%	5.5%		26.7%
American Indian	0.9%	0.9%	1.0%	1.2%		0.4%
Asian	2.6%	4.1%	2.3%	2.1%		2.0%
Native Hawaiian and Other Pacific Islander	0.1%	0.0%	0.1%	0.1%		0.2%
Other	0.2%	0.2%	0.2%	0.2%		0.1%
Two or more races	1.5%	0.8%	1.3%	1.5%		2.2%
Hispanic or Latino	61.2%	71.3%	60.0%	58.3%		55.3%

—-END of Market Survey—-

Summary

1. Residential demand at the zip code level focuses almost entirely on Population growth and Household Formations.
2. Supply is added into the equation so we understand where the market lies in the law of Supply and Demand.
3. Affordability is still dependent on wage growth, but we focus in on household incomes to identify monthly dollar amounts for rent or mortgages.
4. Pull the data for each of the zip codes and line it up side-by-side
5. Score each zip code on a weighted average basis for each quantitative category
6. Start to put together a picture of your target customer with the qualitative data.
7. Drive the zip code and decide which one you think is the best and where you truly want to be working

6

Step 5 - Neighborhood Analysis

"Don't buy the house; buy the neighborhood." −Proverb

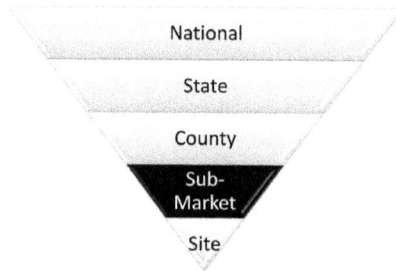

Every neighborhood has a story. Some neighborhoods are known as the "rich" neighborhoods, some are known as the "bad" neighborhoods, and some are simply just suburban or urban neighborhoods. No matter how your neighborhood is generally defined, it is important to find a way to unlock value. Often time people think the "bad" neighborhoods are harder to make a profit than the "good" ones, and that can be true, but the reality is if you improve the area it will add value in some way. It is also much cheaper to get into a "bad" neighborhood and usually costs less to add improvements that will create value.

In my experience, it is actually harder to move into a "rich" neigh-borhood and add more value. I worked on a project located on a waterfront once, and this property was the gateway to a million dollar neighborhood. Unfortunately, the project failed because we did not add enough value. We evaluated the project conservatively and at the time did not have the vision as to what this could truly be and moreover, what it was going to take to be genuinely transformational adding value to such a neighborhood. As we look back today, we can see where the market has gone and understand the opportunity we missed by simply not thinking big enough. We stuck too close to a standard formula and didn't let ourselves venture beyond what we knew as opposed to what was possible...

Assuming you've finally picked your top zip codes, we can focus on very specific neighborhoods and ultimately getting into comparing deals and competitive properties.

One of the tasks from the previous chapter included pulling a list of neighborhoods within the zip codes. It is time to go back to that list and start analyzing the neighborhoods you want to go into. This can be easier said than done depending on your chosen zip code. I have seen anywhere from one or two neighborhoods to 32+ neighborhoods in a single zip code.

As mentioned previously, I've also seen zip codes with no neighbor-hoods. In that case, I would analyze the entire zip code at this level as the demand characteristics are further refined.

Residential demand at the neighborhood level is no longer focused at the easily quantifiable population or household formations growth numbers. Instead, now we look to *desirability-based* demand. What this means is that for residential demand, if money was not an obstacle where you choose to live is driven by the quality of the neighborhood. For families, you would look to a great school system, low crime, and great parks. For singles, you are mainly looking for active nightlife attractions, possibly outdoor activities and likely great restaurants and bars. Depending on your market either demographic group could also be incentivized by proximity to public transit. Understanding, in the real-world, money is an obstacle; we also look at monthly affordability stats through the lens of median household incomes.

What I would say about the analysis at this point is that it is essential to understand deal flow. Without options to buy anything, the best neighborhoods in the world on paper do not mean anything. To that end, I would say it is not unreasonable to "work" anywhere from 5 to 7 neighborhoods at a time looking for deals.

Some zip codes have neighborhoods which are extremely specific and completely different than any other in the city, or they have a cache that gives them a significant advantage. Some zip codes have a bunch of neighborhoods not that different from one another—it's all relative.

There is a way to tell through this market analysis though, so you can prioritize your time and understand what deals are worth chasing and what deals need to be extremely well priced to even look at. The key question to think about as you analyze each neighborhood is thinking to yourself: "What makes this neighborhood unique, why would someone want to live here?"

First, let's analyze the "easy" data going back again to Zillow Research. Go to https://www.zillow.com/research/data/.

The process for pulling and analyzing this data is exactly the same as it was for zip code data we pulled on the previous chapter.

Home Values » Data Type » ZHVI Summary (Current Month) » Geography » Neighborhoods

Then repeat the rental analysis by going back to Zillow Data Research, scroll halfway down the page.

Home Values » Data Type » ZRI Summary: Multifamily, SFR, Condo/Co-Op (Current Month) » Geography » Neighborhoods

Follow all the same steps as before assigning ST, LT, and Stable markets and then comparing the YoY rental rate growth to home valuation growth. I am assuming you set up the formulas from the county and zip code sections by now so I'm not repeating the exact steps here to save you time in reading.

Fix and Flips

Prioritizing again on short-term appreciation if flipping is your business plan, filter for your chosen state then county. Hopefully, at this point, you have the ST Market formula figured out, and you can just insert that next to the neighborhood data; sort in the order of the largest growth ST sub-market.

Then ask yourself the question as to why? Why is this neighborhood doing extremely well? Could you afford to do a fix and flip in this location based on the median home value? How does this fit with the rest of your story you've been developing?

Rental Analysis

Assuming the longer-term buy and hold mentality, if this is your business plan, then I would add in again the LT and Stable Market formulas from the previous sections. Then filter for the largest consistent increases and analyze the data. Make sure to look at the most recent trends to identify if the market is growing, stable, or reverting closer to its longer-term averages? While I would say it is incredibly hard to time the market perfectly, you can use this analysis repeated over quite a few months to identify the trends and buy at the perceived best point. If you are very consistent about tracking your markets and put together a few added charts, they begin to look very similar to stock charts, and it is easier to identify trends.

After you've weeded down to the top 5–7 neighborhoods, the next qualifier I would look for is the actual home value itself. As discussed previously you have to find a market you can afford to play in and be cautious about a market with extremely low values.

Economics Section

The next step in analyzing the neighborhoods is focusing on the data outside of home values. At this point, there are three websites I would utilize for this task. No one site paints a perfectly clear picture, but combining the three adds the most value. Those websites are:

- Onboardnavigator.com *http://www3.onboardnavigator.com/ webcontent/OBWC_Search.aspx?&AID=102&CD_SID=CO001&Frame= 0&Width=600&Height=600&AgentID=&AgentEmail=&SearchID=1& PassBackValues=*
- www.Niche.com
- www.Google.com

I would go through these websites and look up each of your chosen 5–7 neighborhoods individually, focusing on finding the following data and thinking about each in terms of the questions below:

Focus Points

OnBoardNavigator.com key stats:
- **Average household size**: Is this above 2.5 and signaling a more family-centric neighborhood or below 2.0 and signaling more of a singles haven?
- **Population:** What percentage is this of the entire zip code?
- **Households #:** Equates to housing demand.
- **Median household income:** How does this compare to the county and zip code? How does this relate to monthly affordability for renting or owning?

Niche.com key stats:
- **Overall Niche Grade:** This is the accumulation of a lot of great desirability-demand characteristics that are hard to quantify otherwise. Great for comparing one neighborhood vs. another.
- **Overall Public Schools Grade:** If your neighborhood is family-centric I would key in on this Niche grade and category specifically.
- **Overall Crime & Safety Grade**: Whether your neighborhood is family or single-centric, this statistic applies to everyone.
- **Renter-occupied vs. Owner-occupied residences:** Speaks to your breadth of market whichever business model you are pursuing.

Google.com key stats:
- **Transportation:** What are the major arterial lines, i.e., is there a highway five minutes or 30 minutes from this neighborhood? Are there any public transportation options you could purchase property near?
- **Public Features/Parks:** Are there any biking trails, large parks, etc. you want to be located next to? Note: Google will rank the list for you on the left of the map view by reviews posted for all parks in your neighborhood which I would incorporate in your prioritization of which to locate next to.

- **Major Retail Centers/ Intersections:** This speaks to activating the lifestyle in terms of shopping, bars, and restaurants. Housing closer to these centers can be worth more if they are desirable centers.

Once you have pulled all the data, I would score each category based on a weighted average as to which neighborhood had the best result in your opinion centered on your business plan.

My default weightings are:
1. 20% – Household Affordability
2. 20% – Renters or Owners depending on your business model
3. 20% – Overall Niche grade
4. 10% – Median Household Income
5. 10% – Niche grade on Public Schools
6. 10% – Niche grade on Crime & Safety
7. 10% – Niche grade on Good for Families or nightlife depending on your target demographic

Again, the numbers and this analysis will help guide you and give a disciplined and well-informed investment approach, but it will still always come down to the art of the deal to decide where you want to invest.

Below is an exert from my Market Analysis report again for the neighborhood section this time:

Neighborhood Trends:

Summary: Overall analysis shows the top six neighborhoods are all adjacent to each other which points to a general renaissance within the area. Based on my knowledge of the city of Denver, my guess is these are individuals being priced out of the downtown area but needing to stay relatively close. The outlier neighborhood is the 80247 zip code which has the strongest desirability and demographic demand and the best short-term valuations, making it appear as though it is a surging neighborhood. Additionally, I could get into the market at this point with material upside given the average home price is only $229,700 and the Denver county average is $413,500.

I will likely end up working all of the top seven neighborhoods to ensure deal flow, but my prioritization list will go as follows:

1. 80247
2. Villa Park
3. Mar Lee
4. Ruby Hill
5. Athmar Park
6. Valverde
7. Barnum

Home Value appreciation trends:

Based on the valuation trends in each neighborhood it appears the top three markets have phenomenal long-term price appreciation trends with both Villa Park and Barnum showing exceptional YoY growth as well. Barnum and Barnum West also have the best Rent Inc. rankings of the top markets. I'm interested in all of the top five markets, but I'm also still curious about the 80247 zip code/ neighborhood as it ranks number one in the short-term growth markets (as highlighted on the second table) with very affordable housing prices and still very healthy long-term attributes to compliment.

State/County	Neighborhood	Zip Code(s)	A.MoM	A.QoQ	YoY	5Year	10Year	Ave. Home $	Rent Inc.	Rank Rent	LT Mrkt	Values
Colorado		County Ave. -->	0.9%	-1.0%	7.0%	10.9%	6.5%	$413,500	2.0%			
Denver	Villa Park	80204	-2.1%	1.1%	14.7%	20.1%	11.1%	$336,300	2.1%	5	1	
	Valverde	80219, 80223, 80204	-0.4%	5.7%	9.8%	19.3%	10.0%	$297,700	2.2%	4	2	
	Barnum	80219, 80204	-1.2%	0.7%	13.3%	18.2%	10.9%	$305,900	4.1%	1	3	
	Ruby Hill	80219, 80223	1.1%	-0.5%	7.5%	17.2%	8.5%	$319,200	3.8%	3	4	
	Athmar Park	80219, 80223	2.6%	-0.2%	12.3%	16.8%	8.8%	$322,200	0.9%	9	5	
	Barnum West	80219, 80204	-1.2%	-0.5%	14.1%	16.5%	8.9%	$310,000	4.1%	2	6	
	Overland	80223	-1.0%	-3.4%	9.8%	15.8%	8.7%	$375,300	0.9%	8	7	
	Mar Lee	80219	1.5%	0.0%	10.8%	16.3%	8.1%	$315,000	1.4%	7	8	
	Zip Code 80247	80247	2.1%	2.5%	11.5%	15.7%	7.8%	$229,700	1.6%	6	9	
	Montbello	80239	0.0%	-0.1%	7.2%	14.9%	8.1%	$294,800	-0.1%	10	10	

State/County	Neighborhood	Zip Code(s)	A.MoM	A.QoQ	YoY	5Year	10Year	Ave. Home $	Rent Inc.	Rank Rent	ST Mrkt	Values
Colorado		County Ave. -->	0.9%	-1.0%	7.0%	10.9%	6.5%	$413,500	2.0%			
Denver	Villa Park	80204	-2.1%	1.1%	14.7%	20.1%	11.1%	$336,300	2.1%	5	8	
	Valverde	80219, 80223, 80204	-0.4%	5.7%	9.8%	19.3%	10.0%	$297,700	2.2%	4	2	
	Barnum	80219, 80204	-1.2%	0.7%	13.3%	18.2%	10.9%	$305,900	4.1%	1	7	
	Ruby Hill	80219, 80223	1.1%	-0.5%	7.5%	17.2%	8.5%	$319,200	3.8%	3	5	
	Athmar Park	80219, 80223	2.6%	-0.2%	12.3%	16.8%	8.8%	$322,200	0.9%	9	3	
	Barnum West	80219, 80204	-1.2%	-0.5%	14.1%	16.5%	8.9%	$310,000	4.1%	2	9	
	Overland	80223	-1.0%	-3.4%	9.8%	15.8%	8.7%	$375,300	0.9%	8	10	
	Mar Lee	80219	1.5%	0.0%	10.8%	16.3%	8.1%	$315,000	1.4%	7	4	
	Zip Code 80247	80247	2.1%	2.5%	11.5%	15.7%	7.8%	$229,700	1.6%	6	1	
	Montbello	80239	0.0%	-0.1%	7.2%	14.9%	8.1%	$294,800	-0.1%	10	6	

Economic Analysis:

Of the top neighborhoods I reviewed, the first six are all adjacent to each other which speak to their very similar traits across the board. However, zip code 80247 is the standout of all the neighborhoods. They have the highest propensity of renters, the best overall Niche neighborhood grade, the best public schools, the best for families ranking, affordability near the $1,000 mark and a significant population count.

Given the proximity of all the other neighborhoods, I will probably end-up working all of them combined but would likely prioritize Mar lee with the higher affordability, B- Niche grade and a decent number of retail centers close by. This will be followed by Athmar Park then Ruby hill due mainly to their expansive parks. I will need to drive these to make sure they are the right type of parks to be associated with, but from the maps, the higher valued homes seem to border the Platte River.

Neighborhood Demand and Affordability Demographics	Average	Villa Park	Valverde	Barnum	Ruby Hill	Athmar Park	Mar Lee	Zip Code 80247	Weighting
City Name		Denver	Denver	Denver	Denver	Denver	Denver	Denver	
Population	8,986	9,349	4,114	6,357	11,574	9,669	12,851	28,940	
Households	2,855	3,009	1,232	1,854	3,910	3,024	4,102	15,215	
Renter Demand	1,369	1,774	665	1,001	1,877	1,245	1,658	9,396	
Owner Demand	1,492	1,233	567	853	2,033	1,783	2,487	5,636	
Median Household Income	$37,280	$34,411	$28,596	$38,558	$34,004	$43,705	$44,405	$39,838	
Household Affordability	$932	$860	$715	$964	$850	$1,093	$1,110	$996	
Desirability based Demand Traits									
Renter vs. Owner Residences %							Greatest % Owners	Greatest % Renters	
Renters	50%	59%	54%	46%	48%	41%	40%	63%	
Owners	50%	41%	46%	54%	52%	59%	60%	37%	
Percentage of Family Households		Average Households	Average Households	Family Centric	Average Households	Average Households	Average Households	Singles Dominant	
Family Households	35%	33%	39%	46%	31%	35%	39%	19%	
Overall Niche Grade	B	B-	C	C+	C+	B-	B-	A	
Public Schools	C+	C+	C	C+	C	C	C	A	
Crime & Safety	C+	C+	C	C-	C	C	C	C	
Housing	C-	C-	D+	C-	C-	C+	C+	B	
Nightlife	A+	A+	A	A+	A	A	A	A	
Good for Families	C+	C+	C	C+	C+	C+	C+	A	
Diversity	A-	A-	B	A-	A	A-	A	A+	
Jobs	B	B+	B+	B+	B+	B+	B+	B	
Weather	B	B+	B+	B+	B+	B+	B+	C+	
Cost of Living	C+	C	C-	C	C	C+	C	C+	
Health & Fitness	C+	B-	C	C	C	C+	B	A	
Outdoor Activities	A-	A-	A-	A-	A-	A-	A-	A-	
Commute	A-	A-	B+	A-	B+	B+	B+	A-	
Overall Public Schools Grade	C+	C+	C	C+	C	C	C	A	
Best Elementary		Polaris Elbert Elementary	Polaris Elbert Elementary	Polaris Elbert Elementary	Polaris Elbert Elementary	Polaris Elbert Elementary	Polaris Elbert Elementary	Challenge School	
Best Middle School		Dsst: Byers Middle School	Dsst: Byers Middle School	Dsst: Byers Middle School	Dsst: Byers Middle School	Dsst: Byers Middle School	Dsst: Byers Middle School	Challenge School	
Best High School		Dsst: Stapleton high Scho	Dsst: Stapleton high Scho	Dsst: Stapleton high Scho	Dsst: Stapleton high Scho	Dsst: Stapleton high Scho	Dsst: Stapleton high Scho	Cherry Creek high School	
Overall Crime & Safety Grade	C+	C+	C	C-	C	C	C	C	
Assault	52%	13%	145%	45%	41%	67%	1%		
Murder	75%	-100%	-100%	400%	50%	100%	100%		
Rape	-100%	-100%	-100%	-100%	-100%	-100%	-39%		
Robbery	23%	24%	38%	34%	9%	70%	-39%		
Burglary	43%	16%	140%	46%	44%	36%	-21%		
Theft	-20%	-37%	28%	-43%	-32%	10%	-45%		
Motor Vehicle Theft	282%	363%	398%	242%	210%	355%	124%		
List of Major Parks									
1		Lakewood Dry Gulch Park	West Bar Val Wood Park/	Barnum East Park/ 4.1	Ruby Hill Park/ 4.6	Houston Lake Park/ 4.4	Garfield Lake Park/ 4.2	Contry Lane Park/ 4.2	
2		Barnum Mountain Bike Pi	Barnum East Park/ 4.1	Barnum Park Lake Reserv	Denver SW District Parkk	Aspgren Park/ 3.6		Ben Bezoff Park/ 4.2	
3		Paco Sanchez Park South I	Barnum Park Lake Reserv		Sanderson Gulch Park/ 4.	Johnson Habitat Park/ 4.5		Tsistsistas Park/ 4.0	
4					Overland Pond Park/ 3.8	Vanderbilt Park/ 4.4		Cheyenne/ Araphao Park/ 4.4	
5					Overland Golf Course/ 4.	Borders Platte River		Common Ground Golf Course/ 4.2	
Notable Public Transit Stations									
1		Bus Stations line Sheridar	Alameda Light Rail Statior	Bus route on 1st Ave. E/V	Evans light rail station 10	I-25 and Broadway light ri	Bus route on Florida Ave.	Bus route on Mississippi E/W	
2		Bus Stations line 10th Ave	Bus route on Federal Blvd	Bus route on Federal Blvd	Bus route along Evans Av	Bus Route on Exposition I	Bus route on Federal Blvc	Bus route on Havanna N/S	
3			Bus route on 2nd Ave. E/\		Bus route on Federal Blvd	Bus route on Federal Blvc			
4									
5									
Retail Centers/ Intersections									
1		Restaurants at the south i	Retail off Alameda and Zu	Sheridan and Alameda	Federal and jewel	Alameda and Zuni	Mississippi and Morrison	Parker Rd. and Jewell	
2		Retail along Federal Blvd.		Sheridan and 1st Ave	Federal and Evans	Federal and Mississippi	Sheridan and Florida - Lo	Havanna and Jewell	
3				Alameda and Knox	Federal and Florida	Federal and Alameda	Federal and Mississippi -	Havanna and Florida	
4				Federal and Alameda	Klaamath and Evans		Federal and Florida	Havanna and Mississippi	
5				Knox and 1st Ave	Broadway and Evans 15 m			Parker Rd. and Iliff	
Weighted Rank:		2	7	5	6	4	2	1	

—-END of Market Survey—-

Summarizing the Market Analysis

At this point, we have finished the actual market analysis. What I would suggest here is to pause, take a look back at all of your write-ups for each of the steps, read through them again. What is the consistent story that keeps coming out? There should be a common theme throughout as you worked down from one level to the next. It happens more like a puzzle so as the pieces connect; the whole image comes together.

The way I order my market analysis is to have the executive summary at the front so at this point I go back to the beginning and write out the whole story. This should be no more than a few paragraphs – more of an elevator pitch style rather than an essay write-up. The goal in this section should be to come up with a repeatable story you could tell anyone very simply and easily. If you are ready for it, this is what you tell possible investors as well to get them excited about any deals you have on the hook and showcase your expertise in understanding markets.

Below is an exert from the market analysis I have been walking you through along the way where I try to achieve this task along with a summary table of all the facts I have compiled to paint the full picture.

Executive Summary Complete Market Analysis:

The overall national economic sentiment is healthy. GDP is increasing, employment remains very tight, inflation is moderate, and the only visible issue on the horizon is the rise in the federal funds rate which will continue to add pressure to the mortgage rates. This could cause an affordability problem down the line as buyers' ability to pay, and seller's expectations do not match up, putting pressure on residential housing prices in 2019. Time will tell for each market how significant this is based on the demand of those markets.

My chosen state to focus on is Colorado based on having the #1 long-term growth market in the country as well as healthy economic factors across the board. The top county I will focus on will be Denver as it was consistently ranked number 2 for both valuations and economic drivers. However, I will likely look for opportunities in Weld County as well which ranked #1 for economic drivers, especially in the 80631 zip code.

The top zip codes I am going to focus on within Denver County are 80247, 80219, and 80223. Each has strong demand growth and a shortage of supply along with solid 5 and 10year valuation growths. 80247 doesn't have any identified Zillow neighborhoods, so I will focus on the entire zip code for singles and mainly looking to rental properties given 63% are renters with only 19% families and 1.9 members in the average household. For zip-codes 80219 and 80223 I'm going to focus on Villa Park, Mar Lee, Ruby Hill, and Athmar Park. Strong 5 and 10year valuations along with average household sizes at 3+, healthy overall Niche grades for Public Schools and Good for Families make these markets my focus neighborhoods for single-family homes or larger rental units.

Market Analysis Summary Table

Home Valuation Summary		A.MoM	A.QoQ	YoY	5Year	10Year	Ave. Home $	Rent Inc.	Rank Rent	LT Mrkt	Values
State	Colorado	-0.7%	0.2%	6.3%	9.5%	5.1%	$364,600			1	7.3%
County	Denver	0.9%	-1.0%	7.0%	10.9%	6.5%	$413,500	2.0%		2	8.2%
Zip Code 1	80247	2.1%	2.5%	11.5%	15.7%	7.8%	$229,700	1.6%	5	4	11.7%
Zip Code 2	80219	0.4%	0.1%	12.3%	16.5%	8.6%	$313,800	2.4%	1	1	12.5%
Zip Code 3	80223	0.4%	-1.2%	8.5%	15.6%	8.3%	$326,800	2.3%	2	2	12.0%
Neighbor1	Zip Code 80247	2.1%	2.5%	11.5%	15.7%	7.8%	$229,700	1.6%	6	1	11.7%
Neighbor2	Villa Park	-2.1%	1.1%	14.7%	20.1%	11.1%	$336,300	2.1%	5	8	0.5%
Neighbor3	Mar Lee	1.5%	0.0%	10.8%	16.3%	8.1%	$315,000	1.4%	7	4	0.3%
Neighbor4	Ruby Hill	1.1%	-0.5%	7.5%	17.2%	8.5%	$319,200	3.8%	3	5	0.3%
Neighbor5	Athmar Park	2.6%	-0.2%	12.3%	16.8%	8.8%	$322,200	0.9%	9	3	1.3%

State Economics	Employment	Population	Wage Growth	Rank	Top Industry	Weighted Score
Colorado	2.8%	4.4%	3.4%	2	1012 Construction	5.3%

County Economics	HH Formations Growth	Employ. Growth	Pop. Growth	Wage Growth	Weighted Rank	Top Industry	Weighted Score
Denver	3.9%	2.3%	2.6%	6.5%	2	1026 Leisure and hospitality	3.1%

Zip Code Economics	Average	80247	80219	80223
City Name		Denver	Denver	Denver
Population Growth	5.9%	13.9%	1.9%	1.8%
Unemployment Rate	4.1%	4.0%	4.5%	3.9%
Average AGI (Adjusted Gross Income)	1.5%	1.9%	0.7%	2.0%
Household Affordability	$1,012	$1,187	$804	$1,045

Demand vs. Supply Analysis based on Population Growth				
Current Housing Demand	16,476	19,749	21,883	7,796
Current Housing Supply	14,751	15,258	21,399	7,597
Current Housing Shortfall/ (Oversupply)	11.4%	29.4%	2.3%	2.6%
Annual New Housing Needed	1,104	2,753	417	142
Rental Housing	672	1,735	204	77
Owner Occupied Housing	432	1,019	213	65
Annual New Homes being Added	17	11	0	40
Shortfall/ (Oversupply)	1,087	2,742	417	102
New Homes % Shortfall/ Oversupply	7.1%	18.0%	1.9%	1.3%

Neighborhood Economics	Average	Zip Code 80247	Villa Park	Mar Lee	Ruby Hill	Athmar Park
City Name		Denver	Denver	Denver	Denver	Denver
Population	14,477	28,940	9,349	12,851	11,574	9,669
Households	5,852	15,215	3,009	4,102	3,910	3,024
Renter Demand	3,229	9,596	1,774	1,658	1,877	1,239
Owner Demand	2,634	5,636	1,233	2,487	2,033	1,783
Median household income	$39,273	$39,838	$34,411	$44,405	$34,004	$43,705
Household Affordability	$982	$998	$860	$1,110	$850	$1,093

Demand based Desireability Traits						
Renter vs. Owner Residences %		Greatest % Renters		Greatest % Owners		
Renters	50%	63%	59%	40%	48%	41%
Owners	50%	37%	41%	60%	52%	59%
Percentage of Family Households		Singles Dominant	Average Households	Average Households	Average Households	Average Households
Family Households	31%	19%	33%	39%	31%	35%
Overall Niche Grade	B	A	B-	B-	C+	B-
Overall Public Schools Grade	C+	A	C+	C	C	C
Best Elementary		Challenge School	s Elbert Elementary Sr	is Elbert Elementary Scis	Elbert Elementary Ss	Elbert Elementary S
Best Middle School		Challenge School	st: Byers Middle Scho	sst: Byers Middle Schoo	st: Byers Middle Schos	t: Byers Middle Scho
Best High School		Cherry Creek high Sc	Dsst: Stapleton high	Dsst: Stapleton high Sch	Dsst: Stapleton high S	Dsst: Stapleton high
Overall Crime & Safety Grade	C+	C	C+	C	C	C

—-END of Market Survey—-

80

The other step to take is to be sure you have driven these markets. It is easy to do this entire market analysis all online, forgetting the real-world analysis portion which involves old fashioned driving/ walking around. I suggested this be done a couple of times already so if you have done this great, if you have not, now is the time to validate some of the assumptions you've made about each market. Make sure you truly understand the types of markets you are getting involved with and start determining the best areas and the less desirable areas.

Another tip is to do a straightforward analysis online of selling prices or rental rates. For example, go online to a Zillow or Redfin, etc. and type in your neighborhood. Ideally, before you drive the market, then find the areas of higher priced homes or higher rents and lower price points. This will help you map out a route to drive, so you understand the makeup of the neighborhood. Include the parks, transit or retail centers as well. Are the parks in excellent condition or poor condition? Are there a ton of kids running around or a few people sleeping in the middle? Are the transit stations clean or full of graffiti? Are the retailers a good combination of national chains or local entrepreneurs and the condition of the buildings are in good shape? Alternatively, are the buildings in disarray and the retailers of lower-end quality?

The neighborhood you choose to invest within doesn't have to be perfect to make money. This analysis will help you recognize which neighborhood is right for you. The next half of the book is dedicated to utilizing this market analysis in understanding the value of any property and ensuring you make money in whichever neighborhood you choose.

Summary

1. Residential demand at the neighborhood level is based on *desirability* characteristics – where one chooses to live is driven by the quality of the neighborhood.
2. Affordability is analyzed through median household income levels.
3. Pull the data for each of the neighborhoods and line it up side-by-side prioritized on your business plan.
4. Score neighborhoods based on a weighted average basis for each quantitative category.
5. Suggest marking on a Google map all the school districts, transportation nodes, identifying the parks and effectively triangulate your ideal locations.
6. Drive the neighborhoods and decide which one you think is the best and where you truly want to be working.
7. Keep your executive summary short, and to the point, so you can repeat it to anyone with just the essential elements of why you chose your markets.

7

The Market-Based Approach to Analyzing Deals

"Everything is relative in this world, where change alone endures." – Leon Trotsky

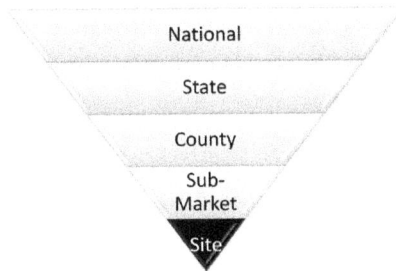

The funny thing about analyzing specific deals and deciding on what one property is worth vs. another; is that it is all relative. The best appraiser in the world is truly just giving their qualified opinion on what a property is worth. Until you sell that property, you will not know. The danger is falling in love with a property and fooling yourself on what it is worth.

Real estate investing is riddled with the bodies of those who have fallen to this concept. I know one specific case where an acquaintance who worked in my office told me all about this property, how great it was, and how he was going to make tons of money on it. I knew the neighborhood this property was in and I was pretty curious how he was going to get his asking price for the flip. When I asked him how he came up with his selling price, he said that he asked a realtor friend of his. I asked if the relator friend worked the market regularly. He said he did not know, but he was a realtor, and they had been friends forever. I asked if he had done his own analysis to know what type of finishes to add and what he could get out of the deal. He said he knew what to do to the house because he had just done the same kitchen and bath at his house.

The fact was, he never looked at the market and truly understood who his customer was. He thought because he liked the finishes in his house, the customer of his flip would like the same thing. While that may be true, that does not mean they will pay the price he needs, and it is not the best way to ensure you maximize value in the market. Understanding the trends of the market by analyzing current listings, backchecking recently sold comps and taking into account qualitative information gathered previously from your market analysis, puts together a much better picture of what you should build in a market.

To that end, at this point you are through the market analysis, you've chosen your neighborhoods to focus on, and you know what is driving value into these areas—it is time to find and evaluate deals. There are entire books written on how to find and evaluate deals because it is complicated and not a clear-cut process—at least often, the best deals are not straightforward. The key to finding and getting deals is all about being creative and resourceful. I'm not going to dive into actually finding deals here, but what I will focus on is evaluating deals from a competitive pricing perspective once you found them.

I start by going back to my market analysis and understanding what type of property I am initially looking for. Specifically, if you chose a market that was great for families, had high average household size, great parks, and great schools, then you should be going for family type units. Generally, this means 3+ bedroom houses or rental units on average.

I then take that information and go back to the listing websites and type in my neighborhood as I did in the chapter before, copying down five or more general price listings or rental rates of the same type such as 3bed 2baths, etc. This helps develop a picture of what the market is likely selling for today for that product. Only take about five to ten minutes to do this exercise, and it will give you a primary starting point to understanding pricing levels in the market. This will also serve as any back of the napkin calculations you may make when scouring the market for deals.

Once that is completed, I start really evaluating deals by using what I call a "soft appraisal" method to analyze deals for both their current value today (used in purchase negotiations) and to help me understand what I think the best price is that I could get for the property post-construction if there were an opportunity to fix it up even as a rental (used for my construction budget and selling price). A professional appraisal is very in depth and takes into account a number of metrics based on an appraisers experience and education on the process. This soft method is definitely more of a "rules-based art." I focus on the bigger items costing a lot of money to fix or can't be fixed at all as those are the most impactful on a local investor's bottom line.

There are a few main points to consider when evaluating a good deal in a market.
1. Location—premium or discount
2. Property condition- advantages or disadvantages
3. Cost of repairs

4. Competitive properties recently sold

Location Premium or Discount

Even within your chosen neighborhood, there are better and worse locations. For instance, you may have a great suburban neighborhood with a park located in the middle. Assuming the park is well maintained and an actual destination spot, then living close to the park will be an advantage and worth a pricing premium. If you are in an urban location, being next to public transportation has an advantage over being a few blocks away—especially when you consider walking in the rain or snow.

The answer to whether you have a great location within a neighborhood is all about going back to your investment story about how you got to this market. In your analysis, what brought you here? If you believe this neighborhood was appreciating quickly because it was located next to a retail location with great bars and shopping, then being located within walking distance to those retailers will be worth a premium.

I would also suggest you should take a look at your potential neighbors. You will not know everything about them, but you can look at the condition of their property and make some judgments about how they maintain their property. Is the lawn well-kept or full of weeds? Do they have chain link fence falling down or is it maintained? If you are looking at a condo, is their balcony full of clutter and their front door adorned with an offensive number of objects? There is any number of traits to glean from looking around and just asking yourself the simple question of who wants to live here? It is also not unheard of or wrong to knock on a few doors when looking at a property. Tell them the truth, you are looking to buy the house or condo in the neighborhood and just wanted to introduce yourself. You may also find someone who was thinking about selling their property but hadn't listed it yet; never know unless you ask.

Understanding the actual streets the property is located on is essential as well. There are certain neighborhoods I like to visit in my city with houses where their front doors practically open to major arterial roads. This means more noise, no guest parking and a lack of privacy. These houses command a material discount to the houses just one street back. I call these homes the "buffer houses." They are usually the cheapest in the neighborhood and do not appreciate the same as the rest of the neighborhood, but they serve a purpose - to buffer the rest of the neighborhood from the noise; value accordingly.

Property—Advantages or Disadvantages

Two general rules here: 1) everything is relative to the market average and 2) It is easy to amend existing square footage (SF), but it is much harder and costly to *add* square footage.

To solve the first rule, the critical part is to become familiar with the type of houses offered in and around this neighborhood; City-Data.com has some general data regarding property age. If the majority of properties in your neighborhood were built in the 50s and you are examining a house built in the 80s, there may be an advantage to work with. However, this could also be a disadvantage depending on the neighborhood. Houses built in the 50s usually have more brick or detail work and less siding which could mean they were built better than a house in the 80s when the cost of building materials was significantly more expensive. Additionally, there may be a look popular with this neighborhood that a house built in the 80s is less desirable in comparison.

Everything is relative. I cannot give hard and fast rules on what is important to your potential customer and what isn't. Again, go back to the story and why people live here. If your story specifically calls out a key advantage of this neighborhood is the assortment of bungalow houses built in the 50s, then a typical 2-story 80s house will command a discount. Note; this does not necessarily mean it is a bad house or you should not go after it. It just means you have to be realistic in your assumptions and understand on the surface; it will go for a discount in the marketplace. This could easily be offset by a location premium or through multiple finish level upgrades such as a new kitchen, master bath, basement, etc., making this 80s property the highest priced in the neighborhood.

The main advantages I often look for when making my value adjustments and identifying the best comps are:

- The sale date of comp—seasonality matters in residential real estate and selling in Q4 and Q1 will cause a discounted price. If the comp sold in December and you are buying in June, you should increase the value of the comp sale price to give you an understanding of where the price would be today.
- The count of bedrooms and bathrooms should be comparable.
- Square footage of the house—this should only represent the finished square footage which excludes unfinished basements.
- Attached or detached parking options and number of spaces included.
- Compare the majority of the exterior, i.e., if the property has siding on 75% or brick on 66%, the market will determine which one is more advantageous than the other.
- Age/condition of the property.
- Kitchen finish level
- Master bath finish level
- Majority flooring type
- Basement finish level

- Heating—baseboard electric is more expensive than natural gas on utility bills, at least in my neck of the woods, so it is worth adjusting if there is a difference between comps as you are not likely to pay to change this.
- Air Conditioning (AC)—this is much easier to add but comes at a hefty cost so central air-conditioning included is worth more than an evaporative cooler any day.
- Lot Quality and size—are the grounds well kept, is there a lot to be desired from landscaping or is it pristine move-in ready. Regarding size, is it a corner lot with half an acre or a house with just a dog-run?
- Sprinkler'd (not a word I know, but it is how myself and many others refer to it)—rather expensive and a pain to put in if there is no sprinkler system.
- Other—always have an "other" category to catch one-offs not typical in the marketplace such as maybe solar power, any easements on the property, pools or playgrounds on the grounds, etc.

2) It is easy to amend existing square footage, but it is much harder and costly to add square footage. If the floor plans are not as open as you'd like, you can usually adjust this—assuming you check with a structural engineer first; this is a great way to add value to the property. However, if basements are critical in the neighborhood and you do not have one, or it is more of a cellar than a true basement, you are not likely to add one, and should assign a realistic discount to your valuation.

This is where the true art of valuing the deal comes in and if it is your first deal it is not a bad idea to work with a realtor experienced in the neighborhood to help develop your assumptions. Next is an example of my "soft appraisal" in action, a few notes to mention here:

- First, all adjustments are made to the subject property. If a comp has a nicer finish then the subject property, give the comp a negative adjustment. If the comp has a lesser finish than the subject property, give the comp a positive adjustment. This part can be confusing so re-read it a couple of times when you start to make adjustments.

- Second, don't assign more than a -5 to a +5% at most for any of these premiums. I have seen quite a bit of "irrational exuberance" when talking with people about what they think the value of their property is. If someone tells you they can get 10% more for just being next to X in the neighborhood, question. Simple math, 10% of a $300,000 property is $30,000 which if this one advantage is that great it may be possible, but that is not a small amount of money to customers. You are always better off being conservative in your estimates to minimize risk on the investment.

- Finally, the dollar amount of the adjustment for all comps is determined by the percentage adjustment assigned multiplied by the sale price of each asset.

The following is the example of my "soft appraisal" on a deal I found in the 80247 zip code based on my market analysis:

You can see from this analysis, post my adjustments I'm valuing the subject property at $338,453 or $183/SF (Top right value under "Adjusted Price $/ SF."). However, the property is listed at $350,000 (Top left value under "Sale Price/ SF") which means we are not in agreement on the surface as to the value of their house in its current condition; though not that far off. That is a significant first step but doesn't yet mean we are willing to pay that price depending on our business plan strategy. This is where we would break this analysis up based on your goals of flipping or renting the property.

Flipping

The next part of the valuation is to see what you believe the property would be worth POST construction if you brought it up to a higher level. That is the comparison I made with the next section of the soft appraisal. This area essentially utilizes the same "rules-based art" to say if it went from a level 2 basement finish to a level 5 it would be worth 4.0% or $16,523 in added value.

Subject Property Current $/SF value ($183.34) »multiplied by 4.0% adjustment »multiplied by post construction SF (2,253)» Equals $16,523.

Comp Rank	Address	Link:	Sale Price/SF	Sale Date	Beds	Baths	Sq. Ft	Majority Exterior	Location	Parking Spaces 1-5	Age/ Cond 1-5	Kitchen Finish 1-5	Master Bath Finish 1-5	Flooring	Basement Finish 1-5	Heating 1-5	AC 1-5	Lot Quality/ Site 1-5	Other 1-5	Sprinkler Y/N	Adjusted Price $/ Sq Ft	Weighted Avr.
Construction Valuation																					$469,686	
Subject Prop.	Chevin Ct 60247		Incremental Adjustments	May 12 1%	4 1%	2.5	2,285 1%	Brick	1	1	1	1	4	5	1b	1%	5 4%	4	3		1	$317.95 SF	

To the same point, it also says if we buy this in November as we expected to do, and take six months to renovate, we would gain $8K due to seasonality alone of selling in May during a higher demand season. This is a tougher concept for some people to grasp that your property could be worth more or less depending on the time of year listed. However, this goes back to the law of Supply and Demand.

People prefer not to move from September to February. If you think about this, it makes sense. Generally, schools of all ages start by August or September, so if you have a family or are a student yourself, you want to be settled before the start of school so you don't have to stress about your living situation for another year. In October-December there are a number of major holidays. Holidays in which gathering with the family is a big deal and having people either come to your place or going to someone else's house is tradition, so people want to be settled in before this hectic time begins. January and February, people are recovering from the holidays and getting their feet under them to start the New Year. All of this is compounded if you live in the northern states and throw snow into the mix. I have moved in the snow a few times, and it is not enjoyable to be cold and uncomfortable lifting heavy objects...

In those months with less demand, prices drop. Where demand outpaces supply, often in the spring and summer months, prices increase. Beyond just understanding this concept, how to adjust for this is the tricky part.

This is another topic you could write an entire book on, but without turning this into a textbook I'm going to give you some basic seasonality curves to work within these appraisals. There are two factors to adjust on the pricing: 1) when you are looking to buy a property compared to when one of the comps sold their property and 2) when you are looking to sell your property compared to when you bought it.

There are six seasonality curves shown next which break out the basic six scenarios. The first number next to "Expected Purchase" represents the month you noted in your soft-appraisal you would purchase your property; in the first example "11" = November.

November is one of the "shoulder" months where seasonal demand is in the middle of the pack with "for sale" housing. As such, any comp you are comparing that sold the previous July for example; you would apply a -2.0% adjustment to that comp. This says if that same property had sold when you were planning on buying your property in November, the comps sale price would have been worth 2.0% less just due to seasonality alone.

Sale Date and Seasonal pricing factor for single family home sales

		Jan	Feb	Mar	Apr	May	Jun	Jul	Aug	Sep	Oct	Nov	Dec
Demand Curve		1	1	3	4	5	6	5	5	3	3	3	2
Expected Purchase	11	2.0%	2.0%		-1.0%	-2.0%	-3.0%	-2.0%	-2.0%				1.0%
Projected Sale	5		2.0%										

The next line to read on this is the "Projected Sale" month. In this scenario, I would buy in November (11) and sell in May of the following year (5). The positive 2.0% is the growth in the market due to seasonality from November to May. If we sell in June, it will be worth 3.0% more. Of course, that also means another month's worth of holding costs which can quickly outweigh the benefits of holding on to a property to time it just right if you are not careful.

The next tables illustrate the other five scenarios of how you would adjust your comp pricing based on the purchase month and what it would do to your pricing based on your projected sale date. There are only six scenarios despite being twelve months as all months with the same curve value have the same curve effect. For example those months with a value of '3' such as November, October, September, and March are all equal and would all have the same curve effects as the previous example curve.

Sale Date and Seasonal pricing factor for single family home sales

		Jan	Feb	Mar	Apr	May	Jun	Jul	Aug	Sep	Oct	Nov	Dec
Demand Curve		1	1	3	4	5	6	5	5	3	3	3	2
Expected Purchase	12	1.0%	1.0%	-1.0%	-2.0%	-3.0%	-4.0%	-3.0%	-3.0%	-1.0%	-1.0%	-1.0%	
Projected Sale	5		3.0%										

Sale Date and Seasonal pricing factor for single family home sales

		Jan	Feb	Mar	Apr	May	Jun	Jul	Aug	Sep	Oct	Nov	Dec
Demand Curve		1	1	3	4	5	6	5	5	3	3	3	2
Expected Purchase	1			-2.0%	-3.0%	-4.0%	-5.0%	-4.0%	-4.0%	-2.0%	-2.0%	-2.0%	-1.0%
Projected Sale	5		4.0%										

Sale Date and Seasonal pricing factor for single family home sales

		Jan	Feb	Mar	Apr	May	Jun	Jul	Aug	Sep	Oct	Nov	Dec
Demand Curve		1	1	3	4	5	6	5	5	3	3	3	2
Expected Purchase	4	3.0%	3.0%	1.0%		-1.0%	-2.0%	-1.0%	-1.0%	1.0%	1.0%	1.0%	2.0%
Projected Sale	5		1.0%										

Sale Date and Seasonal pricing factor for single family home sales

		Jan	Feb	Mar	Apr	May	Jun	Jul	Aug	Sep	Oct	Nov	Dec
Demand Curve		1	1	3	4	5	6	5	5	3	3	3	2
Expected Purchase	5	4.0%	4.0%	2.0%	1.0%		-1.0%			2.0%	2.0%	2.0%	3.0%
Projected Sale	5												

Sale Date and Seasonal pricing factor for single family home sales

		Jan	Feb	Mar	Apr	May	Jun	Jul	Aug	Sep	Oct	Nov	Dec
Demand Curve		1	1	3	4	5	6	5	5	3	3	3	2
Expected Purchase	6	5.0%	5.0%	3.0%	2.0%	1.0%		1.0%	1.0%	3.0%	3.0%	3.0%	4.0%
Projected Sale	5		-1.0%										

These curves are specific to the "for sale" residential market and differ slightly from the "for rent" seasonality curves. However, these curves make sense for roughly 80–85% of the country. Places such as Miami and Arizona have a flatter demand curve as their worst weather and subsequent slower selling times are in the summer through September when it's either hurricane season in Miami or extremely hot in Arizona. Neither of which are times you really want to be moving. Both areas still have the same constraints mentioned earlier about school starts and holidays which is why the curves aren't entirely opposite the national average just less volatile. If you're interested in understanding your specific market demand curve, https://www.nar.realtor/research-and-statistics has decent information on existing home sales at the market level, but usually, you have to buy the reports. That's why I supply the general national curves as a free resource to start with.

The next part of understanding is how to adjust your sales price to when you purchased your property. Again, discussing the soft appraisal example and focusing on the first seasonality curve presented, purchasing the property in November and selling in May of the following year would adjust your selling price up 2.0%. This is how we arrive at the additional $8K in value to your selling price just by timing the market appropriately.

The net value post-construction after all improvements made and factoring in seasonality, is $487,428 or $216/SF. That is a decent margin to the current asking price, but we have yet to add in anything regarding the actual construction budget or holding costs. In today's market, construction is costlier than it has been in the past ten years. That being said, any deal can work if you budget appropriately and buy at the right price.

The best rule of thumb for construction costs and basic holding costs is to assume $20/SF of your property. Note: you have to understand this is just a general swag to help you evaluate deals quickly. If you have experience doing flips in the past, use your data rather than this method, but if you have no experience, this is a good number to start. What you generally can get for that amount is roughly: all new flooring (a mix of carpet and hard surface floors), paint (inside and outside), baseboards, electrical and plumbing fixtures, new kitchen/bathrooms (including cabinets, granite, appliances), blinds or window treatments, and maybe a little bit of landscaping. Should you self-perform the labor, this number only goes further of course.

In this scenario, $20/SF amounts to $45,060. This is a great start, but it should be noted on this strategy I am also growing the finished square footage by finishing out the basement of 407 SF and adding on another bedroom. This is definitely beyond the standard scope of $20/SF but based on the pictures it looks like I will need roughly another $30K to make this transition. I will likely be able to at least add on another half bath down there as well, but until I get into the property, I won't know if the plumbing exists to make that work right now or not. I can always add it, but that starts to inch into the cost/ benefit analysis, so I'm going to initially model without and see if the deal works.

If you are trying to make a minimum 20% return, with $75,060 in construction costs alone without yet digging deeper into my financing or actual construction timeline, you would need to negotiate a purchase price of $314,882 or $171/SF.

Post Const. Value ($487,428) »multiplied by the reciprocal of the minimum return percentage (1-.20 = .80) »less the Const. Budget ($75,060) »Equals $314,882.

This is the negotiating part that will take some work. The $314K is roughly $36K or 10% lower than the asking price which is not out of the realm, but still a stretch unless there is additional motivation on their side to get the deal done. As I'm planning out my negotiation, I would also look at just an 18% return instead of the 20%, which puts the purchase price around $324K and in my mind, an easier sell. Either scenario would leave me with $97K or $87K respectively in gross profit prior to any holding or selling costs.

Post Const. Value ($487,428) »less Const. Budget ($75,060) »less Suggested Offer Price ($314,882)»Equals $97,486.

Post Const. Value ($487,428) »less Const. Budget ($75,060) »less Suggested Offer Price ($324,631)»Equals $87,737.

Renting

With a rental business plan, you are more interested in what the monthly rental rate could be pre and post-construction and what your purchase price needs to be to achieve your returns. To maintain consistency, use the same "soft appraisal" method for this research as well.

Again, all the same, disclaimers are true that this is more of an art than a science and don't get too aggressive with your adjustments in either way. In fact, I kept the same rules for the percentage adjustments as I did with the flipping model. Below is an example of how I would adjust for a rental comp analysis. Note: the adjustments are made to affect the monthly rental rate rather than the purchase price.

From this analysis the suggested rental rate in the market today would be $1,989 or $1.08/SF. The comp list I was able to find had two strong comparable properties, two a little farther out and the final one I used was based on a fully amenitized and professionally managed apartment complex. This is why I also include a weighting section next to the values so you can be sure to emphasize those properties most relevant.

Coming from the institutional level apartment business, I can tell you the highest priced rentals on a $/SF basis are almost always the institutional assets with full amenities and on-site staff. One strategy I have done on my local rentals has been to find a comparable finish level apartment building and set a specific discount to that property as one of my comps.

The reason being, a 300-unit apartment complex will always have vacancies any time of the year and always be your competition. Understanding the percentage gap you believe your property is worth compared to them, gives a consistent benchmark to measure against in the neighborhood. That way no matter what single family comps come up that may change every time, there is always something to go back to as a sanity check when evaluating renewal and new lease rates.

Much like the flipping appraisal previously, this too has a place for post-construction values. However, I have found over the years the scope of work I'm willing to do/need to do for a rental compared to a fix and flip is not the same. At the institutional level, we think in terms of "condo level specs" and "rental level specs." The point is, you can spend more on the condo specs, because your customers are willing to spend more per square foot and because you theoretically will get a much faster return on your money. As such, where I typically use a $20/SF construction budget for my flips, I use only a $10/SF construction budget for my rentals. I also adjust the construction time to no more than three months and ideally two months if I can really press the crew which reduces my anticipated vacancy costs.

Next is my post-construction valuation of how I could improve each component of the subject property.

Comp Rank	Address	Link:	Rent Price/SF		Available Date	Beds	Baths	Sq. Ft	Maturity Exterior	Location 3-5	Parking Spaces 1-5	Age/ Cond 1-5	Kitchen Finish 1-5	Master Bath Finish 1-5	Flooring 1-5	Basement Finish 1-6	Heating 1-5	AC 1-5	Lot Quality/ Size 1-5	Other 1-5	Sprinkler Y/N	Adjusted Price $/Sq. Ft	Weighted Ave.
Construction Valuation																							
Subject Prop.	Chester Ct 80247			Deviation Adjustment	Mar 19 -5%	4	2.5	1,256 3%	Siding	3	3	5	4	2 3%	3	1 3%	5	5	5	1	Y	$2,259 $1.00 SF
Construction Valuation - Adjusted Property Valuation																							
Subject Prop.	Chester Ct 80247			Deviation Adjustment	Mar 19 -3%	4	2.5	1253 3%	Siding	3	3	5	4	1 1%	1	1 3%	5	5	5	1	Y	$468.137 $206 SF

Seasonality again comes into play on this rental appraisal, but the curves are slightly different. Here October through February are the slowest months in leasing where October and November were middle of the pack with "for sale" housing. March through the summertime builds demand nicely, but August is really the last month before demand descends quickly and pricing power falls out from under you.

Here are the five main curve adjustments to use in your soft appraisal analysis similar to what you did in the fix and flip model.

Rental Date and Seasonal pricing factor for rental units

		Jan	Feb	Mar	Apr	May	Jun	Jul	Aug	Sep	Oct	Nov	Dec
Demand Curve		1	1	2	3	4	5	5	4	2	1	1	1
Expected Purchase	11			-1.0%	-2.0%	-3.0%	-4.0%	-4.0%	-3.0%	-1.0%			
Projected Rental	3	1.0%											

Rental Date and Seasonal pricing factor for rental units

		Jan	Feb	Mar	Apr	May	Jun	Jul	Aug	Sep	Oct	Nov	Dec
Demand Curve		1	1	2	3	4	5	5	4	2	1	1	1
Expected Purchase	3	1.0%	1.0%		-1.0%	-2.0%	-3.0%	-3.0%	-2.0%		1.0%	1.0%	1.0%
Projected Rental	3												

Rental Date and Seasonal pricing factor for rental units

		Jan	Feb	Mar	Apr	May	Jun	Jul	Aug	Sep	Oct	Nov	Dec
Demand Curve		1	1	2	3	4	5	5	4	2	1	1	1
Expected Purchase	4	2.0%	2.0%	1.0%		-1.0%	-2.0%	-2.0%	-1.0%	1.0%	2.0%	2.0%	2.0%
Projected Rental	3	-1.0%											

Rental Date and Seasonal pricing factor for rental units

		Jan	Feb	Mar	Apr	May	Jun	Jul	Aug	Sep	Oct	Nov	Dec
Demand Curve		1	1	2	3	4	5	5	4	2	1	1	1
Expected Purchase	5	3.0%	3.0%	2.0%	1.0%		-1.0%	-1.0%		2.0%	3.0%	3.0%	3.0%
Projected Rental	3	-2.0%											

Rental Date and Seasonal pricing factor for rental units

		Jan	Feb	Mar	Apr	May	Jun	Jul	Aug	Sep	Oct	Nov	Dec
Demand Curve		1	1	2	3	4	5	5	4	2	1	1	1
Expected Purchase	6	4.0%	4.0%	3.0%	2.0%	1.0%			1.0%	3.0%	4.0%	4.0%	4.0%
Projected Rental	3	-3.0%											

Remember, the way to look at these curves is to understand, any comp you are comparing that rented the previous August, for example, would receive a -3.0% adjustment. This says if that same comp had rented when you were planning on buying your property in November, the comps rental rate would have been worth 3.0% less just due to seasonality alone.

In my post-construction scenario, I am forecasting construction of three months and then leasing the following month. As such, I add a seasonal curve adjustment of 1% or +$24/ month in rent to account for the difference in timing from my November purchase price to my renting the unit in March.

The model suggests if I'm successful in my upgrades and timing of occupancy, I could get $2,248 /month or $1.00/SF for improving the property (Top right value under "Adjusted Price $/ SF."). Note: the reduction in $/SF from $1.08 to $1.00 despite the rental rate increasing $250/ month is due to finishing out the basement and being able to capture the additional SF in my advertising of the property. From there we can see if this lift in rent is worth it compared to our construction budget based on our cash-on-cash return expectation. The formula is simple:

Post const. rent ($2,248) »less the Current suggested rent ($1,989) » multiplied by 12 months » divided by the return expectation (12%) » In this case, the increase in rent is worth $20,311 in value to the property.

If we use the $10/SF budget of only $18,460, then the first year value creation of $20K is better than the cost of the construction at $18K and represents a safe investment. The concept being, if you had to sell the property immediately for some reason other than market pressures, you should be able to cover your initial investment.

Additionally, if construction only cost $18,460, we would see a 16.8%

return on this rent increase which beats our minimum required return of 12%. This is good; ideally, you want to see a minimum of 10%. This can be lower, but it is important to note that if you take out a loan to cover the construction costs, you want this return to be higher than the interest rate on the loans. If the return is less than the cost of the loan, this increase in rent would actually be costing you money.

The other reality to balance is if you think you can get your full scope of upgrades done for $18K; in this case that will not be possible given the need to build out the basement SF. I'm assuming an additional $24K bare minimum based on the fact the flooring, rough in electric and insulation already exists in the basement. I'll still need framing, drywall, texture, paint, trim and at least one door to finish out the space. This could expand if the plumbing existed or didn't exist for a bathroom addition as well.

If you are curious, the difference from the $30K budget to finish the basement in the fix and flip model to this $24K budget is me cutting materials. Utilizing lower-end flooring, base molding, and lighting options both in count and quality of fixtures, i.e., rental specs vs. condo specs.

Once we run the numbers on a $42K budget, my return drops down to 6.7%. That is going to be tight as I was planning on taking out a second loan to cover the construction costs and I'm not sure I will get it for less than 6.5%. The numbers can still work if you break-even on the loan vs. return analysis so I would keep going with this rental evaluation, understanding this is a red flag to watch.

Should you have to drop your construction budget to make the deal work, you would need to be honest with yourself about what can get done. Understanding, if you cannot turn the basement into a 4, you have to decrease your rental rate value adjustment maybe back to a 2.

Once you do that you have to reset your rent expectation.

Remember this is just a screen and does not account for your operating expenses or analyzing any returns based on the purchase price of the home, debt or equity in the deal, etc. However, rather than put too much work into every deal that comes across, this took me 15 minutes combined to do both evaluations based on information and photos on the web because I have this spreadsheet already set-up and I know this market.

The next step is taking the analysis to the next level of fully under-writing the deal to include operating expenses, purchase price, and financing so you can evaluate the returns and best options for you.

Summary

- There are four main topics to consider when evaluating a good deal in a market.

1. Location—premium or discount
2. Property condition—advantages or disadvantages
3. Cost of repairs
4. Competitive properties just sold

- Utilizing a "soft appraisal" method helps to put the comps on an even basis which will help make your analysis consistent.
- Seasonality matters in this business so pay attention to the timing differences of when you purchase a property and when your comps sold or rented and when you plan to sell or rent the property.
- Always qualify the construction budget rules of thumb with a dose of reality.
- Remember that every deal is as much of an "art" as it is a science. Trust your gut and be honest with your numbers.

8

Proforma Financial modeling and Setting up for Performance

"Everything should be made as simple as possible, but not simpler." – Albert Einstein

Time and time again people seem to get caught up and overwhelmed in the financials of a deal. There are a number of people trying to make things more simplified, but often times when I see these "simpler" models I see major errors. "Back of the envelope" calculations are useful for evaluating many deals quickly, but they are not meant to serve as the long-term underwriting of any deal. For that, you need to put in the time and truly understand the market and your property as well as the financials to put the whole picture together.

This chapter was developed to show you how to do the underwriting and give you visual examples as well as definitions of each category to make it as simple as I could. Some of this may seem overwhelming at first but take your time, and you can work through this to come up with a way of understanding the value of your investment and help reduce your risk on any deal.

Remember, if you have trouble seeing any of the example tables presented in this book, go to the website: www.neighborhoodsuncovered.com and download the pdf of the completed market analysis.

Both strategies of either the fix and flip model or rental model can be valuable, but it all comes down to what you want/expect to receive as financial returns for each investment. I have read a number of books discussing what the authors believe are acceptable returns on each business model. However, I have not seen much consistency as to how people calculate these returns. I've seen numbers from 10–50% "returns," but when you dive into them, those numbers are often based on Internal Rate of Returns (IRR's) or Cash-on-Cash returns which seem to be used interchangeably in some cases... Note: these are not the same thing. One is used to evaluate the value of an investment over the life of the investment (IRR). The other is used to evaluate the value of the investment at one specific period in time (Cash-on-Cash). Irrespective of which business model you pursue, you need to project short-term monthly cash-flows and long-term project cash-flows to calculate your true returns on the project.

In the institutional world, we always set up *proforma* models. If you are not familiar with that term, it just means a financial model used to project forward financial measures. In the case of real estate we use it to forecast forward expected cash flows including revenue and expenses, calculating monthly and annual financial returns on our investments.

I have talked with more than a few local investors who only create a one-time, one month or one year snapshot of what they think their revenue and expenses will be. This means they never trend growing expenses or growing revenues or include any one-time events to understand the effects of these events on your overall returns.

This is a mistake; it is essential to at least project forward your revenues and expenses a few years to identify the trends and understand any significant impacts. For instance, on the rental business plan, you need to project forward your monthly operating expenses and model in the effects of vacancy when a customer moves out. Most customers only stay in a rental for an average of two years, so over a three to five-year time period, you will have some vacancy and have to turn the unit. Hopefully, the previous customer's deposit will cover any significant turn costs, but sometimes it is good to model in a few extra dollars to be conservative.

Flipping Proforma Model

Flipping is a short-term game by definition, but still, I like to plan out monthly cash flows to understand how each expense category is being affected. It is worth analyzing a market appreciation factor in your holding time during the flip if you are in a hot market. Hopefully, through this analysis, you found a property in a fast appreciating sub-market, so you have the potential to increase your returns by simply holding the property for six months. The bottom line you need to get to is an understanding of what returns are acceptable to you and working the numbers forward and backward to arrive at what your purchase price and construction budget have to be to get you there.

The proceeding image is an example of a proforma model I set up based on the deal discussed in the previous chapter and influenced by the market analysis.

Monthly Fix and Flip P&L		Purchase Month1	Construction Month2	Construction Month3	Construction Month4	Construction Month5	Construction Month6	Construction Month7	Construction Month8	Sale Month9	Month10	Month11	Month12	Year1
Variables	Monthly $ Values	Nov-18	Dec-18	Jan-19	Feb-19	Mar-19	Apr-19	May-19	Jun-19	Jul-19	Aug-19	Sep-19	Oct-19	
	Other Income	$0	$0	$0	$0	$0	$0	$0	$0	$0	$0	$0	$0	$0
	Effective Gross Income (EGI)	$0	$0	$0	$0	$0	$0	$0	$0	$0	$0	$0	$0	$0
$.80 /sf	Utilities	$92	$92	$92	$92	$92	$92	$92	$92	$92	$0	$0	$0	$738
$10	Marketing	$10	$0	$0	$0	$0	$60	$60	$60	$0	$0	$0	$0	$180
$38	Insurance	$38	$38	$38	$38	$38	$38	$38	$38	$38	$0	$0	$0	$304
0.0%	Real Estate Taxes	$139	$139	$139	$139	$139	$139	$139	$139	$139	$0	$0	$0	$1,108
	Other Expenses	$0	$0	$0	$0	$0	$0	$0	$0	$0	$0	$0	$0	$0
3.0%	Sales Commission	$0	$0	$0	$0	$0	$0	$0	$0	$15,451	$0	$0	$0	$15,451
$500	Model Furniture Cost	$500	$0	$0	$0	$0	$0	$0	$250	$250	$0	$0	$0	$500
1.0%	Other Selling Costs	$0	$0	$0	$0	$0	$0	$0	$0	$5,150	$0	$0	$0	$5,150
	Operating Expenses (OE)	$779	$269	$269	$269	$269	$329	$329	$579	$21,120	$0	$0	$0	$23,432
	Net Operating Income (NOI)	($779)	($269)	($269)	($269)	($269)	($329)	($329)	($579)	($21,120)	$0	$0	$0	($23,432)
Yes	1st Loan	$2,019	$2,019	$2,019	$2,019	$2,019	$2,019	$2,019	$2,019	$267,691	$0	$0	$0	$281,824
	2nd Loan	$482	$482	$482	$482	$482	$482	$482	$482	$43,966	$0	$0	$0	$47,339
	3rd Loan	$0	$0	$0	$0	$0	$0	$0	$0	$0	$0	$0	$0	$0
$75,060	Construction Budget	$12,510	$12,510	$12,510	$12,510	$12,510	$12,510	$12,510	$0	$0	$0	$0	$0	$75,060
	Operating Free Cash Flow/ BTCF	($15,790)	($15,280)	($15,280)	($15,280)	($15,280)	($15,340)	($15,340)	($3,080)	($312,777)	$0	$0	$0	($427,855)
Property appreciation in the market monthly and annually														Year1
Date of Purchase	Nov-18	Dec-18	Jan-19	Feb-19	Mar-19	Apr-19	May-19	Jun-19	Jul-19	Aug-19	Sep-19	Oct-19	
Home Value	$314,882	$338,453	$333,384	$325,355	$325,294	$337,595	$348,368	$515,022	$515,022	$0	$0	$0	$515,022
Home Value Appreciation		$23,571	$18,502	$10,473	$10,411	$22,713	$33,485	$200,140	$200,140	$0	$0	$0	$200,140
Seasonal / Market Adjustment		-1.5%	-2.4%	0.0%	3.6%	3.2%	2.7%	3.2%	-1.7%	0.0%	0.0%	0.0%	43.56%
1st Loan - Principal		$456	$457	$459	$461	$462	$464	$466	$468	$0	$0	$0	$3,693
2nd Loan - Principal		$0	$0	$0	$0	$0	$0	$0	$0	$0	$0	$0	$0
3rd Loan - Principal		$0	$0	$0	$0	$0	$0	$0	$0	$0	$0	$0	$0
Total Property Cash Value		$24,027	$18,959	$10,932	$10,872	$23,175	$33,949	$200,606	$200,608	$0	$0	$0	$203,833
Property Sale Net Profit		33,649	13,757	(9,062)	(23,973)	(26,549)	(30,653)	193,389	91,060	0	0	0	91,060
Contributed Equity		$5,000	$5,000	$5,000	$5,000	$5,000	$5,000	$5,000	$5,000	$0	$0	$0	$5,000
Property Sale Net Profit + Equity		38,649	18,757	(4,062)	(18,973)	(21,549)	(25,653)	138,389	96,060	0	0	0	96,060

In the example here, I have an assumption for each of the major revenue and expense categories on the left side, but I time their cash flows differently in some instances. In a flip, there isn't going to be much revenue coming in prior to the sale of the property unless you can get creative. However, there is never a shortage of expenses as outlined below.

- Utilities – Will be paid by you until the house sells, so it is just an average straight-lined assumption
- Marketing - I would not start until about two months prior to construction ending.
- Insurance – Is a straight-lined monthly assumption until the property sells.
- Real Estate Taxes – Are modeled as straight-lined for simplicity, but likely will be prorated for the remainder of the fiscal year when you purchase the property.
- Other Expenses – Simply a catch-all for anything else needed to add for any specific deal such as HOA's as an example.
- Sales Commissions and Other Selling Costs - Modeled as a percentage of the sales price that applies at the sale of the property.
- Model Furniture Costs –A nice to have in showing the property, so I usually model two months of rental costs on the furniture.

This first section will outline the operating cash flows of the deal and leave you with a Net Operating Income (NOI) line item. The next section includes debt and capital items such as the construction budget.

- Loans/Debt – Depending on how the deal is structured, you may have any number of loans from banks, private equity investment sources, friends and family, etc. Here I model out the monthly debt payments and account for the balloon payment at the end when the property is sold.
- The Construction budget - This is just straight-lined for modeling purposes. You can set up a side model to discuss drawing down bank loans and the actual timing of cash flows if need be. Depending on the loan structure it can pay to time out the cash flows to reduce the interest paid on costly short-term debt.

The combination of NOI less debt and capital expenses leads to Operating Cash Flow/ BTCF (Before Tax Cash Flow). This represents the money you will make prior to paying Capital Gains taxes or Business Entity Taxes. This is the critical line item you really need to get to in a financial model. Far too often people stop at NOI or they mesh the two categories together and call it NOI vs. Cash Flow. Either way, this is how one would break out the model at the institutional level and is often missing at the local investor level. It is worth mentioning that I'm not going to go into the additional calculation for taxable income. I would suggest you consult an accountant for the specifics on that information.

The next section walks you through property appreciation utilizing the growth rates from the market analysis and tracks your equity in the deal.

- ***Home Value*** – Tracks the original purchase price on the deal and what the property should be worth based on market growth.

1. Day one, you track the actual purchase price paid.

2. Month one, you increase the value to what you identified as the true market value based on your soft appraisal. If for some reason you overpaid compared to the true market value than you would decrease to that value instead.
3. The next part adds in market growth.
4. The final adjustment is when you complete construction. You should add in the post-construction value assumed from your soft appraisal.

Note: add in the difference in total dollars on top of the market growth. Using my 80247 example we did the soft appraisal for and modeled here in the proforma if the post-construction value is $487,428 you would subtract out the current value of the property identified (not necessarily what you paid) of $338,453 to come up with a difference of $148,975; use this dollar amount to add on top of the market growth. The reason is because this value too should have grown with time as the market grew and this method incorporates that growth rather than handcuffing you to the $487K figure. In the example above, when I actually plan to list the property, it should be worth roughly $515K due to seasonality timing and the market growth factor.

- **Home Value Appreciation** – This bullet is the difference between the anticipated home value and your purchase price showing the anticipated accrued equity in the deal.
- **Seasonal Adjustment** – Calls out the difference in seasonality from when you buy to when you sell the property. It goes back to the economics of supply and demand I noted earlier in the book. Seasonality is a very real factor that can absolutely affect your property value solely based on the timing of your purchase or sale.
- **Loan Principals** – If you are using amortizing loans than you should track principal payments paying down the property as equity as well. On a flip, this will be minimal based on how long you hold the investment, but on a rental, this can grow to a decent figure.

The sum of this section highlights your growth in overall anticipated monthly cash value on the deal.

When you take your Operating Cash Flow/ BTCF »Plus your Total Property Cash Value, you come up with the Property Sale Net Profit. This would give you the total value creation on the deal if you sold the property on any given month, including paying off all your loans (as applicable) but does not include your own contributed equity. I find it helpful to break out my equity to understand the actual profit of the deal.

The final line item of Property Sale Net Profit PLUS Equity adds in the initial and on-going equity contributed into the deal. These last two line items are essential to flippers as you look to find out the total cash you will make on any deal when you sell.

Now that we have outlined the proforma model and described each line item let's walk through the specifics of this example to help illustrate this in practice.

The monthly NOI of this fix and flip deal shows losing roughly $270-$330 per month on utilities, insurance RE taxes, and marketing while under construction. The final two months of my holding period increase with the model furniture costs and then ultimately the anticipated selling costs. The net NOI for the entire nine-month holding period is a loss of $23,432. This is typical of fix and flips as you rarely have any revenue coming in to offset the monthly costs.

I modeled a loan payment based on 6.0% APR with a 30-year amortization, 2% up-front, at 70% (Loan-to-Value) of Post-Construction value. This effectively covered $31K of my construction costs and I would be able to take out a second/ private equity loan for the remaining $44K at 10% APR with 2% up-front again. Note: I modeled paying off the balance of the loans (less construction costs so as not to double count the cost) on the month I sell the property.

All-in, this investment will cost $427,655 to hold for nine months. Now we have to balance the costs out with our projected selling price based on the market appreciation and post-construction valuation.

Conservatively, I am modeling the market rate growth on this one at the annualized QoQ rate of only 2.45%. The reason being is due to the short-term nature of the hold and that when we did the market analysis it was clear both the MoM and the QoQ numbers were much lower than the YoY number for the state and every sub-market and neighborhood we analyzed. This could be a warning sign of a market slow down and so we would want to hedge our risk in assumptions by utilizing the slower rates. One of the benefits of great timing and taking advantage of seasonality, is over the specific nine months shown, the 2.45% annualized growth equates to a forecasted project growth of 5.7%. This is greater than the YoY growth as the project is timed perfectly to realize market growth on the appreciation of the project without hardly any negative seasonality coming in July through October.

Note; my numbers in the 'Home Value' line show I purchased the property for $314K; on month one I jump the home valuation up to what I value it at today of $338K. Once construction is finished, I jump it up to my post-construction value plus nine months appreciation.

The rest of the section only adds back in any principal payments made on the debt which over the nine months equated to only $3.7K, but it helps.

The net of the proforma suggests I would sell the house for $515,022 less my costs of $427,655 would give me a profit of $91,060. Now on this scenario, since my two loans would pay for the purchase price, holding costs and construction, I only added in $5,000 equity for miscellaneous expenses and my initial equity on the deal. As such, my returns on this deal are pretty good, but so good I would not use traditional financial metrics to evaluate. The important thing to compare here is the $91K cash—before taxes. Is that enough for you to spend the next nine months stressing and possibly fighting with every construction company you work with?

In my mind, this is a good deal, and I could stop the analysis here picking up the phone to go after it. However, since I'm also interested in rental investments, I want to take the analysis in that direction to compare so I can evaluate what the most profitable business plan would be for this opportunity.

Rental Proforma Model

The rental business plan is a long-term game, and while appreciation is essential, it won't be realized for quite some time since the property will not be sold for 3, 5, or 10+ years. The critical understanding here is the growth possibility of the monthly rent and controlling the monthly operating and turn expenses.

Monthly rental rate growth is very dependent on the quality of the property as established in the soft appraisal analysis, but also based on general market growth. The catch here is understanding again, real estate is a seasonal business, and you can maximize the rental rate growth in the spring and summer. To that end, I want to give you a tip that in my experience of pricing over 50,000 multifamily units, the single most impactful factor to maximizing rental rate growth is *lease management.*

If you've never heard of this term, I'm not surprised. For some reason, very few experts at the local real estate level understand this practice. Lease management is essentially just ensuring you write the lease lengths of your tenants to end in the best months to release the unit—generally the summer. A unit sitting vacant is a killer to financial returns and can take years to repair the damage of one to two months of vacancy to your finances. Practicing disciplined lease management helps to reduce vacancy time by matching the supply in the market with the highest customer demand in the market.

This concept directly ties to the seasonality discussion we've already had, but I always recommend leases end in April or May. This allows time to turn the unit and ensure even if it does not pre-lease before the current tenant moves out, I can have confidence it will rent within a few weeks. Additionally, May is the peak of pricing power in most markets. After May, there ends up being so much supply in the market from June through August, prices only decrease from there. Especially, as many people will drop their rates to ensure they fill up by the end of August understanding if they don't, they could be sitting on a vacant unit for much longer. This is where it is worth evaluating opportunity costs and understanding if it is worth taking less per month than the last lease just to get someone in through the winter. Then you can write a shorter-term lease to have their lease expire in the April/May time period where you can bring their rent up to market rates or replace them with someone else.

There is a reality you cannot control everything, and if a customer breaks their lease early, hopefully, you can collect enough in fees to pay for the extra time your unit sits vacant if it is in the slower months. Just be sure to write the next lease to end in the spring/summer months.

The point is, all of this needs to factor into your pro forma model to understand when your customers move-in and move out matters to your bottom-line. Expenses, however, are less seasonal aside from utilities, but maintaining efficient operating costs only improves margins and reduces the risk of losses. No big secret or surprise here, it is pretty straightforward. Pass off utilities of the property to your customer on top of their monthly rent; if you can charge them extra for parking because the property is in an urban or supply constrained market, great. Pretty much everything else needs to be controlled by you to maximize profits.

Next, is an example of the rental proforma I put together for the 80247 project we have been discussing. I won't go through the specifics of each line item again as they are the same as the fix and flip model we just covered previously.

In this model, I'm still assuming a basic level of construction to bring the property up to the market average. As such I do not show any revenue coming in until the fourth month. This means renting in March which is in-line with my preference to lease in the spring and summer months.

The rental rate is also based on a post-construction value which I timed out for three months with the reduced scope and my marketing maxed for all three months in an effort to pre-lease the unit for a move-in the day after I complete construction. Utilities only come into play when the unit is vacant and again I straight-lined the construction budget cash flow. Even though I am doing construction, I still plan for a monthly budget on additional repairs and maintenance of the property. In this model since I live close enough to the property, I am not planning to have a mgmt. company. This is always my preference as my expectations for operations usually far exceed what most one-off management companies can provide. I have unfortunately gone through quite a few management companies...

The debt payments on this property account for two loans. The first is based on a 70% LTV of the current listed value of the property at $350K, not my purchase price. This is a 4.5% APR, fully amortized loan, with a 30-year amortization and 1%/point up-front.

The second loan is for the construction costs of $42K with a 7.0% APR, interest-only loan, on a 15-year amortization and 2% up-front.

The monthly NOI comes out to roughly a positive $2,032 per month in the first year once construction ends and I lease up the property. However, I am modeling putting long-term debt on this property as well as adding an on-going monthly capital reserve bucket of money for large expenses such as water heaters going out, etc. The net Operating Free Cash Flow/ BTCF suggests a monthly profit of $369 once leased in the first year.

I do not show the monthly details between each year, but essentially every two years I model a move-out with a month's worth of vacancy carrying out the model for five years. With this scenario, I don't model selling the property as I did in the flipping model as I plan on holding rentals for 5+ years.

Since I'm not planning on selling, the lower section showing the appreciation of the property is important but plays less into my rental analysis as the property needs to stand on its own from a monthly cash flow perspective. It's also important to note my post construction home value is about $60K less than the fix and flip model. There are a few reasons for this. 1) I am cutting my construction budget and doing lower end finishes which then lowers the value. 2) I'm using a more conservative 10yr market growth rate on this rental proforma vs. the YoY growth rate on the fix and flip proforma. 3) Seasonality and timing of the year is in March vs. May. These are the type of small adjustments that have significant impacts on your underwriting.

The net of this proforma over a 5year holding period, without a sale, puts the IRR (Internal Rate of Return) at -48% which essentially says this investment does not pay for itself over a five-year horizon.

Now if I assume a sale at the end of year five, it changes everything, suddenly my IRR jumps to a positive 28%. This is generally how rental property value creation works. Therefore, the way I would look at this is first to ensure the monthly cash flow had enough of a cushion to ride out any significant issues. The second would be to ensure I felt relatively confident about my market growth assumptions, as that is clearly where the real value is on this deal. If I feel confident in both of those than this deal is pretty enticing from a long-term buy and hold perspective. Again, this is where doing the market analysis and following this book can add significant value to your investment.

The bottom line is this; all these adjustments both positive and negative will help you once again come up with a story about this investment; why someone would live here, why it is worth more than the property down the street, which business plan is the best, and ultimately why it is going to give you an X% return on your money and efforts.

Summary

1. It is important to create a monthly proforma for the entire anticipated investment horizon.
2. Utilize market growth rates identified in your market analysis to support the property appreciation values and applicable selling price or rental rate projections—this is fundamental to profes-sional underwriting.
3. Lease management is a key to maximizing your financial returns as seasonality matters in the real estate business.
4. Finally, financial models are just assumptions, so make sure you understand the story behind these assumptions and document them at the time of underwriting. This is so you can look back on them throughout your investment and use them as a guide as well as a measuring stick on performance.

9

Pricing for Re-sale, Pricing for Rentals

"Intelligent people make decisions based on opportunity costs." – Charlie Munger

Going back to the story of my co-worker I introduced in chapter 7; sometime later, I asked him how the flip was going. He told me he was just about finished, but he was frustrated is realtor friend suggested a lower price. He decided he was going to keep his original underwriting and see how it went.

A month or so later he came to my office and asked for my help and give him my honest opinion on his price. I opened up his listing, and in two seconds you could see he was $15K above all other houses in the area. When I pointed it out, he said he knew that, but that was the price needed to make the deal work and he'd already come down $30K! I asked how long he could hold on to this price before he started losing money on the deal. He said one more month. I suggested it takes thirty days to close on a property so at this point he was already there in terms of losing money. He said the house was worth every penny and he knew someone would take it at this price. After all, it was a bargain having come down $30K in price already...

A month later the property had still not sold. He finally had to drop the price even lower than the $15K just to get out of the deal. Without knowing all the specifics of the deal, I can tell you he lost quite a bit. All because he received bad advice going into the deal and wouldn't face the reality that the market will pay what the market will pay. People have alternatives to your property, it pays to do your homework at the beginning of an investment, but don't back yourself into a corner where you do not have any wiggle room should conditions change.

In the last chapter, we discussed underwriting for returns which assumed operational holding costs of the asset. If you were flipping this may be anything from 3 to 12 months or if it is a rental they are on-going for the life of the investment. Either way, they have a material impact on your bottom line profitability.

One of the biggest mistakes I see people making is not pricing their investment appropriately with the market. I regularly hear of people holding out for more money on a deal and ending up washing away the entire gain with monthly holding costs as the property sits vacant. Pricing the asset optimally is often the trickiest part of any deal because it can make or break your returns.

Flips

Usually, about a month to two months from the end of construction, depending on the progression of construction, you are usually getting the property ready for sale, which first and foremost includes identifying the price. The first step along these lines is to go back to your "soft appraisal" method I discussed a few chapters earlier and identify all the updated recent comp sales in your sub-market similar to your property; the catch here is to be honest with yourself. When you went into the deal, your kitchen design might have been intended to be rated a 5 out of 5 on the scale. However, when you got into the flip, you found something unexpected and your budget got crushed. This seeped into your kitchen design, and now it is really a 3 or 4 rather than a 5. Be honest. The market will not care what you intended to do and will only punish you if the price of your asset is too high.

Once you have identified 3–5 comps and come up with a price based on the numbers, listen to those numbers. You have to be careful here not to jump them up, so you can make more on the deal because your expenses slipped. Again, the market will pay what the market thinks the property is worth; nobody cares if your construction budget slipped. Now that being said I do not think its a terrible strategy to start a little higher and work your way back, but you have to build in time and a strategy for how that will work.

One strategy that seems to work well is starting roughly 3–5% higher than your soft appraisal suggests about a month out from being ready. Gauge the interest; if your market is hot, you should still be able to pull in some decent interest even though you haven't much to show. However, I would never be afraid to give a "hard-hat" tour and walk someone through a 90% complete property. My rule of thumb is that the flooring should be in, even if it is covered with protection; generally, this means it is in good enough shape to show.

If after that month you do not have a commitment I would drop it 3%, hold for 2-3 more weeks gauging the interest and then drop it another 3% if it does not work. Assuming your market has not gone cold, and you were honest with yourself in the soft appraisal method, that should be enough to work. After that, I would drop it roughly 2%-3% every 2–3 weeks thereafter as holding costs and the opportunity costs of not being able to redeploy the capital in another investment become more-costly than taking the hit on the price for this investment. However, it is all relative. There is no perfect formula and if you are in-experienced, working with a knowledgeable realtor can really help this part out. Just make sure when you pick a realtor they are willing to work on selling your property, not just listing, printing a few flyers and hoping that works. Hope is not a strategy...

Rentals

With rentals, if you are selling the asset, then the process is exactly the same as above with the flip. However, the process of re-renting the property is more complicated when it comes to determining the right price, as holding costs are typically far more impactful to your bottom line.

The first step whether you are offering your current tenant a renewal or planning to re-rent the space is to run another soft appraisal as before on the rental rate comps in the sub-market. Here again, it will pay dividends to be honest with yourself. However, this can be more of a moving target as you are competing against the comp set of today, not when you bought the property. As such the market or units available today may have changed, and your finishes which were a 3 previously are now a 2. Conversely, you may have upgraded to what you thought would have been a 4, but today it is a 5 in the market based on what's available. The point is, your customers will be looking around the market at their other options to rent, so you need to be aware of those options and price accordingly. Once you have your price, I would run through the math and understand the opportunity costs of that price.

Initially, the equation for weighing opportunity costs for renewals is the same as new leases. This is because here you are just looking at how long the payback period will be to pay off the initial anticipated vacancy loss.

Here is what I always do to check before requiring an increase. Add up your typical monthly holding costs such as debt payments, Mgmt.

Company, insurance, repairs account, taxes, capital account, etc. Then add in one-time marketing costs if the unit goes vacant along with your turn costs and less the deposit from the existing customer. Ideally, the deposit covers the turn costs, but not always unfortunately, so you need to think through if this turn will require more work than normal to make this unit rentable again and add that additional cost into the equation. The sum of those costs equals your "1st Month Vacancy Costs." They represent all the costs you have to pay the first month your current customer vacates.

Next, figure out your renewal offer rate/ new lease rental rate. This rate should equal the market rate for your property based on the soft appraisal analysis noted above from the previous chapter - updated for this time period of course. Subtract out the typical monthly holding costs used above (NOT including one-time marketing costs or turn costs) to come up with your anticipated monthly Free Cash Flow (FCF) with the proposed rent amount.

In general, I assume it will take a month to move-in a new customer if I get the unit back from April to August. This makes the formula much easier as you simply divide the 1st Month Vacancy Costs by the anticipated monthly FCF to arrive at how many months of occupancy it will take to pay back the initial month worth of vacancy loss.

$$\frac{\text{1st Month Vacancy Costs}}{\text{Free Cash Flow}} = \text{\# of Months to Payback Vacancy Loss}$$

There is no hard and fast rule as to what number you are looking for, but in general, the payback period should be less than you anticipate writing the next lease term for. Otherwise, you run the risk of the new customer moving out again before you paid back the first vacancy loss and then you could incur another vacancy loss. This leads to a money-losing venture on the operating side.

Here is a snapshot of how I evaluate the deals:

Monthly Rental Rate Evaluation	
Holding costs	$1,891
Marketing Costs	$150
Turn costs	$800
Deposit	$800
1st Month Vacancy Costs	$2,041
Prospective Monthly Rent	$2,299
Holding costs	$1,891
Average Monthly NOI	$408
Date Vacancy Started	4/1/2019
New Move In Date	5/1/2019
Days Vacant	30
Months of Occupancy needed to pay off Vacancy Loss	5.0

For renewals only, I would take this evaluation to the next level as I would also look at how long before I started to realize the gains from my new increased rent. You see the first equation just told you how long before you paid off the vacancy loss, but not how long before you started to realize the increase.

In the illustration I show next, it shows the proposed new rent compared to the current rent and identifies the net Monthly Revenue Increase – in this case, $111. If you believe it will take you a month to re-lease the unit, you would divide the 1st Month Vacancy Costs noted in the previous illustration at $2,041, by the anticipated Monthly Revenue Increase. This will give you how many months of occupancy it will take for you to pay back the vacancy loss AND begin to realize the rent increase.

Renewal Break-Even Evaluation		
Prospective Monthly Rent	$2,299	
Current Monthly Rent	$2,188	5.1%
Monthly Revenue Increase	$111	
Months at Prospective Rent to Break-Even on the increase		18.4

Here again, there is not necessarily a hard and fast rule as to what the "right" number is, but I would look for it to be less than two years.

Fun fact, the average rental customer stays roughly two years and the larger the square footage, the longer they stay! There is a loose "direct correlation" between how much stuff you have compared to the length of time you stay in one place. i.e., moving is a pain. Therefore, I would look for this number to stay below 24 months and the farther below, the better.

In conclusion of evaluating increases, if your payback period on the initial vacancy loss is less than your anticipated next lease term and/or your break-even period on the increase is less than two years, I would consider it a worthwhile risk to take the increase. If one or both of those are not the case, I would play with the increase to see what you would need to be able to achieve on the monthly rent to make it worthwhile. Then check your gut if you really believe you could get that rate in the market or if your customer will pay that rate. Sometimes on renewals, it is worth going out with the increased rate and negotiating with your renter to avoid the vacancy loss altogether and arriving somewhere in the middle on the increase. At least you know you are profiting from the very next month if they stay, even if it is not all the increase you wanted compared to waiting two years to realize the increase.

To be clear, this does not mean you are losing money or not making any money while you are below the break-even point, it just means if the market rent is growing, you don't realize any additional profitability until after the break-even stay.

What this all adds up to is the importance of pre-leasing a unit. Every day of vacancy costs money and shortening the time from move-out to move-in can add serious value to the bottom line. This is where pricing the unit right is crucial; getting $50 more per month may not make sense if the unit sits for another 10-15 days...

Also, I would suggest showing the unit to prospective tenants before the current tenant has moved out.

In Manhattan, the market is so tight, and occupancy is so critical to the financial success of any investment, showing an occupied unit is a common and accepted practice. Most other places across the country; this is just odd; however, I do not see why. As long as you check the local laws, write the lease appropriately, and schedule appointments for showings, there is nothing wrong with this practice. The major caveat here is, understanding you cannot control the condition of the unit at the time of showing, even if you wrote into the lease that they must keep their place "show ready," picked-up and cleaned once they have given notice to leave. So, if your tenant is questionable or you know there is a significant amount of work to be done, this will not work out well for you. Aside from those instances, I think it is a great practice and gives far better odds to lease the space faster and generate profitability.

Summary

1. Pricing the investment for re-sale on a flip or rental is crucial to your profitability.
2. Being greedy can cost you everything on a flip or time on a rental.
3. Refresh the soft appraisal every time you need to price the asset and be honest with yourself.
4. Look at the opportunity costs to create your strategy and understand how long you can hold the price before it starts to cost more than the benefit of the increase.
5. If the payback period on a rental increase is less than the next anticipated lease term, it is likely worth the risk.
6. If the break-even period on a renewal increase is less than a two-year lease term, it is likely worth the risk as well.
7. Always try to pre-lease the rental unit or pre-sell the flip!

10

Concluding Summary

"In summary, all great work is the fruit of patience and perseverance, combined with tenacious concentration on a subject over a period of months or years." – Santiago Ramon y Cajal

The bottom line is this: consistency and self-discipline are the keys to investment success. Throughout this book, I have given you a consistent, repeatable process helping you find the best markets for you to invest in as well as a process for evaluating those deals to maximize your investment. The self-discipline to do the analysis is up to you. My hope is that I've given an easy enough process once you've set it up, making it much easier and efficient to utilize.

To that end, as I mentioned early on in this book, I've also created a spreadsheet anybody can use with this exact process already well defined and built-in. You have seen examples of it throughout this book in every exert where I posted a table of data as the example; there is also far more to the spreadsheet tool I did not discuss here.

This custom-made spreadsheet helps you organize all of the data throughout the market analysis which is often the hardest part of the entire process and took me years to develop and perfect. You can benefit from my experience and save yourself a lot of time with this tool.

What the spreadsheet includes:
1. State analysis – Home Valuation and Economic Data
2. County analysis – Home Valuation and Economic Data
3. Zip code analysis – Home Valuation and Economic Data
4. Neighborhood analysis – Home Valuation and Economic Data
5. Purchase valuation—"soft appraisal."
6. Rental rate valuation—"soft appraisal."
7. Proforma financial modeling (includes seasonality calculations)
8. Summary of financial returns
9. Rental rate evaluations of new leases and renewals
10. Additional resources for online supply and demand websites

This tool will walk you step by step through the process discussed here in the book to take any uncertainty out of the process. For those less financially inclined, all of the formulas are already done for you. In many of the sections you can simply paste a data table, and the formulas will produce the answers instantly. Where there are additional inputs specific to your investment, there is commentary and instructions to walk you through each number. Even if you are financially inclined, this is a great resource to save you time and give you a consistent, repeatable process you can do again and again to maximize profits and reduce risk.

Here is the link to my website so you can look through and decide if it makes sense for you: www.neighborhoodsuncovered.com . Additionally, on my website, I have a market analysis outline which was the basis of all the examples throughout the book in the Market Analysis chapters.

Here is my email, if you have any issues or questions about the book or the spreadsheet, or outline, please do not hesitate to contact me: J.Dimond@neighborhoodsuncovered.com

Finally, as you worked through this book I hope you were able to identify some of these main takeaways:

1. The market analysis starts at the broadest level and funnels its way down to each deal.

2. Every investment has a "story" which is based on an investment thesis telling any investor why you, and they, should choose this deal over all other deals.

3. Frequency: the national and state analysis need not be done more than twice a year, but I would update the counties once a quarter and the zip codes or neighborhoods once a month. Tracking the changes over time will help you identify trends not easily uncovered the first time you pull the data.

4. The home valuation screen is a great place to start for each section of the analysis as property appreciation is the number #1 criteria a local investor is looking for.

5. The economic data tells the top-line story of why the home valuations are growing as they are.

6. Some of the qualitative data can be just as important as the quantitative data; helping define your target customer and position your product to appeal to the greatest number of buyer/renters.

7. Evaluating deals is as much of an "art" as it is a science. Be sure to trust your gut on any deal and be honest with yourself as you adjust the numbers.

8. Once you come up with a decision, stick to it. If the numbers do not fall in-line during negotiations to what you need/want, do not be afraid to walk away. You're doing this analysis to help understand what an investment is worth; don't ignore it in the heat of the negotiation.

9. When pricing a property for sale or rental, don't be greedy. The opportunity cost of having a vacant unit can far outweigh modest gains in price very quickly.

10. Have fun, I know this is analysis and economics, but think of it almost as uncovering a lost treasure as you dig through the data to

identify the best investment for yourself. If you stick to the story and are consistent in the process, I have no doubt you will uncover the perfect neighborhood.

I hope you have enjoyed the book! If you did enjoy it, please leave a rating. I'm shooting for only 5's so if something is taking your rating down from there, please send me an email and let me see if I can address your concerns before you rate. I want you to be as successful as possible.

Thank you, and good luck.

THE END

Appendix: Supply and Demand Links

This section gives you additional resources above and beyond what is listed in the book. Most of these are free resources as well, but some are paid subscriptions. Again I do not make any money on these links. They are the accumulation of years of conducting market analysis and tracking sites that were useful to me.

Disclaimer: Neighborhoods Uncovered, LLC or the author of this book have no responsibility for the persistence or accuracy of URLs for external or third-party Internet Websites referred to in this publication and does not guarantee that any content on such Websites is, or will remain, accurate or appropriate.

DEMAND DATA

Bureau of the Census
Economic Census
https://www.census.gov/programs-surveys/economic-census.html
Income
https://www.census.gov/topics/income-poverty/income.html
Construction
http://www.census.gov/mcd/index.html
Governments
http://www.census.gov/govs/www/index.html
Manufacturing/Mining
http://www.census.gov/mcd/index.html
Retail trade

http://www.census.gov/econ/www/retmenu.html

Services

https://www.census.gov/econ/services.html

Transportation

https://www.census.gov/econ/isp/sampler.php?naicscode=48-49&naicslevel=2

Wholesale trade

https://www.census.gov/wholesale/index.html

International trade

http://www.census.gov/foreign-trade/www/

Estimates

https://www.census.gov/programs-surveys/popest.html

Projections

https://census.gov/topics/population/population-projections.html

Population Profile

https://www.census.gov/geo/maps-data/maps/thematic.html

State, quick county facts

https://www.census.gov/quickfacts/

CenStats Databases

https://www.census.gov/data/data-tools/censtats.html

Building Permits by municipality

https://www.census.gov/construction/bps/

County business patterns

https://www.census.gov/programs-surveys/cbp/data.html

USA Counties

https://www.census.gov/support/USACdataDownloads.html

Detailed Occupation (race,sex)

https://www.census.gov/people/io/

American FactFinder

https://factfinder.census.gov/faces/nav/jsf/pages/index.xhtml?_ts=515934302510

Reference Maps

http://factfinder.census.gov/servlet/ReferenceMapFramesetServlet?

_lang=en
  Thematic Maps
  https://factfinder.census.gov/faces/nav/jsf/pages/what_we_
provide.xhtml?page=tmaps
  Census 2000 Special Equal Employment Opportunity (EEO) Tabula-
tion
  http://www.census.gov/hhes/www/eeoindex.html
  Population estimates
  https://www.census.gov/data/developers/data-sets/popest-popproj/
popest.html
  TIGER (Topologically Integrated Geographic Encoding and Referenc-
ing system)
  http://www.census.gov/geo/www/tiger/
  Landview 6 (mapping software)
  http://www.census.gov/geo/landview/

  Bureau of Labor Statistics
  Employment & Unemployment
  http://www.bls.gov/bls/employment.htm
  National Employment
  http://www.bls.gov/ces/home.htm
  National Unemployment Rate
  http://www.bls.gov/cps/home.htm
  U.S. Economy at a Glance
  http://www.bls.gov/eag/eag.us.htm
  Employment Projections
  http://www.bls.gov/emp/home.htm
  Job Openings and Labor Turnover
  http://www.bls.gov/emp/home.htm
  Employment by Occupation
  http://www.bls.gov/oes/home.htm
  Business Employment Dynamics
  http://www.bls.gov/bdm/home.htm

Wages, Earnings, & Benefits
http://www.bls.gov/bls/wages.htm
Wages by Area and Occupation
http://www.bls.gov/bls/blswage.htm
Earnings by Industry
http://www.bls.gov/ces/home.htm
Employment Costs
http://www.bls.gov/ncs/ect/home.htm
Employment Projections
http://www.bls.gov/emp/home.htm
Geo. Profile of Employment and Unempl.
http://www.bls.gov/gps/home.htm
Regions, States, and Areas at a Glance
http://www.bls.gov/eag/home.htm
Industries at a Glance
http://www.bls.gov/eag/home.htm
State and Local Employment
http://www.bls.gov/sae/home.htm
State and Local Unemployment Rates
http://www.bls.gov/lau/home.htm
Mass Layoffs
http://www.bls.gov/mls/home.htm
State and County Employment and Wages
http://www.bls.gov/cew/home.htm
Bureau of Economic Analysis
Personal Income/ Outlays
https://bea.gov/newsreleases/national/pi/pinewsrelease.htm
Regional Input-Output Multipliers
https://www.bea.gov/regional/rims/rimsii/
Survey of Current Business
https://bea.gov/scb/
BEA Overview of Economy
https://bea.gov/newsreleases/glance.htm

State and Local Personal Income
https://bea.gov/regional/index.htm
State of the Cities Data Systems, HUD (economic performance indicators for metro areas, including demographics, employment, and crime)
https://www.huduser.gov/portal/datasets/socds.html
HUD home page
http://www.hud.gov/
Policy Development and Research Info Service
http://www.huduser.org/
American Housing Survey
http://www.huduser.org/datasets/ahs.html
Assisted Housing: Natl./Local
http://www.huduser.org/datasets/assthsg.html
Fair market Rents
http://www.huduser.org/datasets/fmr.html
Low-Income Housing Tax Credits
http://www.huduser.org/datasets/lihtc.html
Qualified Census Tract and
http://www.huduser.org/datasets/qct.html

SUPPLY DATA

CB Richard Ellis (office, industrial, retail)
http://www.cbre.com/
CB Richard Ellis
http://www.cbre.com/research-and-reports/featured-reports-global
Colliers
http://www.colliers.com/Corporate/MarketReports/
CRESA (industrial)
http://www.cresapartners.com/
CoStar (office, industrial)
http://www.costargroup.com

Cushman Wakefield (office, industrial)
http://www.cushmanwakefield.com/en/research-and-insight/
Delta Assoc.(office, Ind., lodging, multi, retail))
http://www.deltaassociates.com/
Ernst & Young (global RE markets)
http://www.ey.com/gl/en/services/strategic-growth-markets
Ernst & Young RE, Hospitality & Construction
http://www.ey.com/us/en/industries/real-estate
Ernst & Young Natl. lodging forecast
http://www.ey.com/global/Content.nsf/US/Media_-_Release_-_01-28-03DC
Dodge/McGraw Hill (construction outlook)
https://www.construction.com/
Marcus & Millichamp MSA sector research
http://www.marcusmillichap.com/research/researchreports
Meyers Group (residential)
http://www.meyergrouppresidential.com/
MPF Research (apartment)
http://www.mpfresearch.com/
FRED (monthly supply of houses in the US)
https://fred.stlouisfed.org/series/MSACSRNSA
NAI (market info)
http://naibusinessproperties.com/market-research/
ONCOR (office market)
http://www.oncor.com/EN/Pages/default.aspx
PKF Online (hospitality)
http://www.pkf.com/services/hotel-consulting/
Price Waterhouse Cooper
http://www.pwc.com/us/en/asset-management/real-estate.html
REIS (pay for data/ free analysis)
http://www.reis.com/subscriptions/national.cfm
Smith Travel Research (lodging)
http://www.strglobal.com/

Society of Industrial and Office Realtors
http://www.sior.com/
Staubach (office, Ind., retail)
http://www.staubach.com/knowledgecenter.asp
TCN (market report, reviews)
http://www.tcnworldwide.com/reresources.cfm
CBRE (free research)
https://www.cbre-ea.com/
Grubb-Ellis Quarterly market sector trends
http://www.ngkf.com/home/research/us-market-reports.aspx
Grubb-Ellis Quarterly Metro trends
http://www.grubb-ellis.com/Research/ResearchLocalResearch.asp?
UserGroupID=&LinkID=101&ParentLinkID=58
Landauer (office, multi, Ind., retail, lodging)
http://www.grubb-ellis.com/Financial/ServiceFinancial.asp?UserGroupID=
&LinkID=11&ParentLinkID=0
Jones Lang LaSalle (market, listings, construction)
http://www.joneslanglasalle.com/
Chain Store Guide (fee)
http://www.csgis.com/
Commercial Property News
https://www.cpexecutive.com/
National RE Investor news
http://www.nreionline.com/
National Apartment Assoc (vacancies, etc)
https://www.naahq.org/
Natl. Assoc of Homebuilders
http://www.nahb.org/
Natl. Assoc. of Industrial and Office Properties
http://www.naiop.org/
Intl. Council of Shopping Centers
http://www.icsc.org/
Builder Online

http://www.builderonline.com/
RERC
http://www.rerc.com/

ECONOMIC AND OTHER DATA

FRED (Federal Reserve Economic Development)
https://fred.stlouisfed.org/
Wells Fargo Monthly Economic Forecast
https://www.wellsfargo.com/com/insights/economics/monthly-outlook/
Livingston Survey of Prof. Forecasters
https://www.philadelphiafed.org/research-and-data/real-time-center/livingston-survey/
Trading Economics.com
https://tradingeconomics.com/united-states/gdp-growth-annual
Kiplinger Survey
https://www.kiplinger.com/article/business/T019-C000-S010-gdp-growth-rate-and-forecast.html
Regional Economic Conditions (FDIC)
https://www.fdic.gov/bank/analytical/stateprofile/
City Data
http://www.city-data.com
Economagic.com
http://www.economagic.com/
Data Ferrett
http://dataferrett.census.gov/TheDataWeb/index.html
The Association of University Business and Economic Researchers
https://auber.org/
Real Estate Economics Abstract Search
http://www.areuea.org/publications/ree/search.phtml
Grubb-Ellis Regional Econ. Forecasts
http://www.ngkf.com/home/research/about-our-research.aspx
Global Insight (Wharton/WEFA) (industry)

http://www.globalinsight.com/

enter on Budget and Policy Priorities(state)

http://www.cbpp.org/state/

Federal Housing Finance Board (affordable housing, monthly interest rate survey – mortgage data)

https://www.fhfa.gov/

Mortgage Bankers Assoc.

http://www.mbaa.org/

Natl. Assoc of REITs

(cap rates)

http://www.nareit.com/home.cfm

Natl. Council of RE Investment Fiduciaries

http://www.ncreif.com/

Business Outlook Survey

https://www.philadelphiafed.org/research-and-data/regional-economy/business-outlook-survey/

MACRO economic Survey of Professional Forecasters

https://www.philadelphiafed.org/research-and-data/real-time-center/survey-of-professional-forecasters/

Integrated Public Use Micro Data Series

http://www.ipums.umn.edu/

FedStats

https://fedstats.sites.usa.gov/

Woods and Poole (MSA data and projections/fee)

http://www.woodsandpoole.com/

American Demographics (news/subscription)

http://www.americandemographics.com/

Natl. Low Income Housing Coalition

http://nlihc.org/

Biz Sites selection tool(demographics for fee)

http://www.bizsitesdata.com/

Asset Dev. Institute (State Demographics)

http://www.centeronhunger.org/ADI/adistate.html

Beacon Hill State Competitiveness Report
http://www.beaconhill.org/MasterDocumentSCI_A1.pdf
Economist Outlook (seasonality discussions)
http://economistsoutlook.blogs.realtor.org/2014/09/02/autumn-and-winter-slowdown/
Economist Outlook (seasonally adjusted vs. not)
http://economistsoutlook.blogs.realtor.org/2017/01/17/comparison-of-seasonally-and-not-seasonally-adjusted-existing-home-sales/
FRED (median sales price of houses in the US)
https://fred.stlouisfed.org/series/MSPNHSUS